SELECTED POEMS

Also by Roger Garfitt from Carcanet

Given Ground

ROGER GARFITT

SELECTED POEMS

Penrith
November 11ᵗʰ '00

CARCANET

First published in 2000 by
Carcanet Press Limited
4th Floor, Conavon Court
12-16 Blackfriars Street
Manchester M3 5BQ

A CIP catalogue record for this book
is available from the British Library
ISBN 1 85754 479 X

The publisher acknowledges financial assistance
from the Arts Council of England

Set in 10pt Garamond Simoncini by Bryan Williamson, Frome
Printed and bound in England by SRP Ltd, Exeter

to David Harsent

Acknowledgements

Acknowledgements are due to the editors of the following magazines and anthologies, where the new poems and extracts from journals were first published:

Along the Line, Brando's Hat, Earth Ascending, The New Exeter Book of Riddles, Leaves at the World's Edge, London Magazine, Making Connections – poems for Matt Simpson, The Path from the Year's Height, PN Review, Obsessed with Pipework, Resurgence, Stand, and *Writing in Education.*

'El Día del Amor' and 'Vivir Pobre' first appeared in *Granta* as part of 'Notes from Abroad'.

'Living in Colombia' first appeared in *London Review of Books* as part of 'Where Colombia Screwed Up'.

'Walking Off the Fear' and 'The Flying Horse' first appeared in *Travelling on Sunshine* (Artists' Agency, 1996), the book of the Blyth Residency, which was the second prizewinner in the 1997 Raymond Williams Community Publishing Prize.

'From the Ridge' was commissioned by the Poetry Society under their Poetry Places scheme. The performing version with Sue Harris on the dulcimer was first presented at Ver Poets.

'Footsteps on a Path', 'The Workshop in the Quarry', 'Jack the Lad', 'The Spirit of Lumley Hall', and 'Working through Resistance' were commissioned by Shropshire County Council Arts Service as part of their Rural Links project.

'The Country Over My Shoulder' first appeared in *Poetry Review.*

Presences of Jazz was first performed with the John Williams Septet at the 1999 Ledbury Poetry Festival.

In All My Holy Mountain was commissioned by the Arts Council of England for jazz settings by Nikki Iles and first performed with the composer and the John Williams Septet as part of the 1999 Season of Music at Leasowes Bank.

Border Songs were commissioned by Shropshire County Council Arts Service and engraved on glass screens in the County Records & Research Centre, Shrewsbury. The commission fee was paid by The Wilfred Owen Association. The glass engraver was Janice Howe and the artist in charge of the project was Steve Field of the Public Art Resource Unit in Dudley. They were published in a signed limited edition by Five Seasons Press. The performing version with Sue Harris on the dulcimer was first heard on BBC Radio 4's *Kaleidoscope.*

Contents

New Poems and Extracts from Journals

From inside my eyes, looking out

From inside my eyes, looking out,
I see your eyes, black from the doorlight,
quiver to silver
as they follow your fingertip trace
my cheekbone visor.

From inside my eyes, looking in,
I see that my head is a wedge
splitting your breastbone.
You may trace embroideries down its grey edge
and not mist the iron.

If you stop, your gaze coming to meet me,
I will hide my eyes, turn them aside
to the air:
and yet you, refusing my desire,
felt unfair:
as if my eyes, tactful in their redoubt,
seemed gentle to you,
from inside yourself, looking out.

The Third Time

To build an edifice
          and the base is rotten
To build it again, honestly, gingerly
          it gives way again
To rebuild now, the third time, slowly,
to place each brick in the fear
that somehow it cannot stand

          is work for the damned.

By the Parks

Just discernible in twilight
a slow movement
a child on his bicycle
carving spirals down the broad path

Very slow
pedals pressed to a nicety
the maestro
approaches

For Lesley

      The last thing touched me
the way you said
            Oh, and Roger . . .
and for a moment
           laid yourself against me

      Before I thought to kiss your cheek
you were gone

      In the street next to yours
a flood of yellow rose

In the Georgian street
           the next one to mine
I found a whole cluster
          small roses
of a deep red

      This house will never miss one

I searched the full flowers

                     for one
still tense

                     Ah, there!
I reached

       snicked it carefully
at the base of the stem

       I found my smallest glass
       washed off every stain
       dried it with a hand of cloth

Now the bud is alive

                     in clear glass
       one petal

                     seems to burn

Animula

Light things,
that never know their own mind
from one minute to the next,

forage in chinks on the city wall;
their grafts take in rotted wood,
in fallen leaves:

goldfinches plunder between the copings
along Rose Place; hawthorn and dogrose
flower in the sump of a willow.

And all this time I was teaching you
the earth's tables, the long divisions
of frost, you had the wits of a bird,

your songs would break from the dark haulm:
for you are mineral in a moth's wing,
rain in the wind or air in the bone,

11

you are swift and lark; in you the elder
seasons move, from flower to berry,
and the north meets the westron wind.

Here I come now, my heart in my boots,
ignorant of anything
beyond the ache of mammal and clay.

Hares Boxing
for Nigel Wells

This way and that
goes the runaway furrow.
Nose to tail
goes the tunnel
in the grass.

Now the leader
swivels, jerks up his heels.
The trick flickers
along the rope of hares:
heels over head they go, head over heels.

It's the Saturday
after Valentine:
in Florey's Stores
the kids go
into huddles,

Oh! What did he put?
Go on, tell us! we *promise*
we won't tell.

Did she send you one?
        Did she?

Over the winter nothing has changed
but the land. The hedgerows
are in heaps for burning.
The owl's tree stands vacant
between the scars of smooth earth.

The sunlight falls on cleared spaces,
on the old lines. The hares meet
as they met before Enclosure, far out
in the drift of grasses, their fisticuffs
like tricks of the eye.

What catches the light, what the eye believes
is the rufous shoulder, the chest's white blaze:
what it sees are up on their haunches
the blaze throw its guard up, the shoulder
slide in a punch; two pugs that duel

stripped to the waist by sunlight.
And the Fancy? They emerge
from the corners of the eye, low company
from the lie of the land, with guineas
in their stare, without visible means.

The purse is all he fancies. The generations
bunch in his arm.
Toora-li-ooral go the fifes in his blood.
As tall, as straight as a thistle,
Jack Hare squares up to Dancing Jack.

Spring Grazing

The bullocks back and churn in a mill by the gate.
Their breath hangs in snarls on the unravelling mist.
They balk at the open field.

Birth was a lean-to shed, opening off the womb,
a lamp's heat in a bright puddle on the straw,
suckling fingers, a slant of milk in a bucket.

Winter was the next shed along, a press of flanks
jostling from the hayrack to the hissing water.
Above them, the empty socket of a lamp,
a sun as cold as tin: by four they had thinned
to a tread, a breath, a sense sifting the darkness.

The crib suited them. Over the hocks in fetid litter,
they blinked at cold snaps, breathing their own thick air.
When ice gagged the tap, or gales jemmied at the slates,
they tore at summer, tangling, spilling from the rack,
bit on June, crushed July, mouthed August in the cud.
They boned up, angular as hangers in their coats:
contentment repacked them into hummocks of fat.
After five months' swaddling, the seven months of lean:

day broke. In a hurl of shouts, a jabber of sticks and slaps,
their world blew inside-out. The three dimensions ripped,
and their three successors roar: frost, glare, the East Wind.
The herd breaks. They've no mind for this, only the gap
mind was, a crater where the instincts wheel and scream.
The stampede circles, treads out circle on circle,
makes the womb, makes the lamp, makes the magic of heat.
Between tramping hooves, a shadow rebuilds the dark.

A season of surfaces, of a climate thin
as sun's warmth in the topsoil, night's degree of frost:
but the herd are banked ashes, a broad ramp of flame.
Bay, rosebay, red roan: the gods of bronze return
into iron land. They are blind as a landslide,
as simple as the tides. Heads dip, breathe scents of grass.
In their nerves of straw, in their hay brains, a sweet spark
kindles. The appetites sing in their bonfire coats.

14

Dark becomes shade, shelter; the trees, an air like water;
the barn holds bales of silence: the long days begin
– though herds adrift in their green dimension, their minds
the line of the wind, the slow digestion of light,
are imprinted on ten square yards. They graze patches
the size of their winter shed, areas they know.

What lines the mirror of the fields of light? Instinct
has an eye on the silence, an ear for the dark.

Titchwell

Far as your eyes or mine can see,
the waves' sinuous symmetries
flex and stretch towards the shore,
a silt accretion, featureless as air,
whose histories are winds, whose flora sea birds' cries.
These dunes are where the abstract takes its exercise.

Sand gathers grass. Mud grows samphire.
The seven silences of water
turn to the one silence of earth.
Here elements cross seasons, death crosses birth.
The rabbits' summer-runs surface from winter shoals,
their warrens strewn with tide wrack, skate's eggs, broken shells.

The marsh horizons part. We see,
in tide's ebb flow, in shore wind's lee,
the crescent estuary grow
to half a moon of land. The noon shadow
flickers and shape-shifts over it, a fluent band
translating heat into furlongs of dry, white sand.

Though dwarf shapes paddle at our feet,
ringed-plovers' bell notes, prompt wingbeat,
spell our gigantic trespass here,
declare distinct proprieties of fear.
Terns hang like slender toy kites, shrieking their anger.
Black-backed gulls glide off-shore, exact spans of danger.

Equinox

Heads down now the hard weather's come, the kids
snap out of school. At four the greengrocer
stacks his pavement spread, trolleys it inside.

No sunset. The sky at chromatic north.
No cloud, only this north wind of colour,
the sun's recessional, the equinox,
when fire and brimstone behave like angels.

Low, impermanent as a shanty-town
lie the bare precincts, the dormitory streets
to these trebles of gold, this green alto.

Over the playing fields, at the street's end,
the cold declensions of October light.

Winter Economy

The horse turns its tail
into the flailing wind.

The labouring crow
is pitched over the oak
and heaves to on a fence post.

Under the hissing trees
the lank cattle,
their coats greased with wet,
roll the night's hay
in cud through their molars,
chewing over a patch of thunder in June.

Carnage

Remnants of fur
cancelled by a wheel,
the tread of successive tyres
franked into the patch on the road,
we're inured to those:
a ridge of pelt
flickers in the gusts of morning traffic . . .
What was it?
Clues blacken, smear,
the riddle is ironed flat.
Under rush hour
the bristles fray halfway to dirt,
join the dropped oil rag,
the scorch of exhaust,
mysteries briefer than skidmarks.

But this is raw,
its clue is butchery, a dumb
mouthing of blood.

It spins into the fast lane
and lies there, quartered meat.

Shock perhaps, the muscles locked
and couldn't run . . .
the detail sets in the kerb,
a perfect cast of terror:
the muscles grip like cogs,
the nerves are wire
– the ability to adapt
improves with death.

What hammers on is primitive,
the ancestral spite: this chunk
a car punted across the A.40
is combustible still, its cells
detonate heat.

The stump, the abdominal animal,
pumps, and its new mouth
snarls blood:

but air has breached the pump,
night frost will temper this blood,
whose batteries pulse at the arrest;

steam pushes into the headlights.

The Hitch-Hiker

One hand crabs along the seat back,
prising a grip; one sensory foot
hovers down, testing the floor,
testing the temperature. He hangs
over the seat, as over a piping bath,
inching himself down.

There's a knife-edge brim on his old felt,
his muffler ties as neatly as silk:
of his natty dress, only the skills remain.
Nothing else's quite right: a hold-all for shopping,
trousers frayed at the knee. Old vanities
are the best he can do.

Alone at a bus stop, on the verge of the by-pass:
these are the Home Counties of the Moon. The present
starves him in its thin atmosphere. Death
is coming over him like a yawn.
He hitched a lift, his admission of exile
a shy elocution of the thumb.

He's talked himself down to the seat.
He muffs the door shut. I edge into gear
as he perches there, brittle, hollow-boned.
He settles back, and identity rises in him
– he's got his second wind. He remarks,
'You're nowhere without a car these days,
are you?'

Strix

1

mutter in the rafters
cursing in mid-air

Maurice up a ladder
flush against the straw stack
George up on his toes
on the top bar of a hurdle

snipping at the netting overhead

Maurice's hands pressed together
the ends of flight feathers
flattened between his wrists

Keep still, you silly beggar,
or I'll have your foot off!

Barn Owl, says Maurice

hanging upside down
claws caught in the net
that keeps the birds from the grain

stretched on his toes
George edges the scissors
past the two-inch talons

Let go then, you beggar!

2

It's very dark for a Barn Owl . . .
flecks of ginger down its breast
in the ruffs round its eyes

Tawny! says George
Not round enough, is he, in the face?
Barn Owl's more round, sort of clock-faced.

3

hunched
just as his hands left it
in the back of the open trailer

Must be pretty giddy
– well, would be giddiness in humans

then it squirts

a long squirt of yellow slime

slumps against the side of the trailer

the sun shines full into the open barn
onto the tin where it lies
into its open eyes

in the light
they are bruises of blue
bruised flints
liver blue

the inner eyelid
sweeps up across the eye
as if the sun was a smear of dust

George spreads a paper sack
over the edge of the trailer

the sun is a tear in the sack
a mark
that gleams on the feathers of its head

Best gather it up, p'rhaps,
put it in the back of the hay barn

I close one hand on its feet
on those eight sickle claws
the other on its wings
and lift

it's no weight

4
its head turns
scans the tractor shed, the thin shadows

it lets itself be carried

I walk under the hay barn
towards the roof's line of shadow
across the floor
towards the bales
stepped against the sky

one flick
lifts it from my hands
one beat
skims it into the shade

I watch its downward, lapsing flight
flick and glide, flick and glide

it drives headfirst into the stack
crams between two bales
and is still

a sparrow flits down from the rafters
flits back

it's well hidden

mottlings merged with the grass heads
its dandelion and clover
baled with the hay

B Roads

Once they had the future taped.
Once they were just a blueprint
in their father's eye.

Long ago all the nonsense
was knocked out of them.
Now they've settled for good,

and don't doubt they are needed:
a sequence of pressures
has made them what they are.

Something in the City
is serious business,
black pinstripe, or plain grey.

(In the country they wear
pepper and salt, are known
by unclassified names.)

Day in, day out they have
their shoulder to the wheel.
Their nose is the grindstone.

Gradually they come
to quiet conclusions.
They turn to history,

in the *striae* of the Ice Age
find lasting company,
their heroes in the dead stars.

The Emperor Hadrian's Farewell to his Soul
after the Latin
written on his deathbed

animula, vagula, blandula,
hospes comesque corporis,
quae nunc abibis in loca,
pallidula, rigida, nudula,
nec ut soles dabis iocos?

Little whit, wit o' the wisp, little soul, little solo,
– such company! my blood's brother, genial air –
don't you know where you're off to?
Lych land, unhoused, below zero.
Better change your ways. Nothing to laugh at there.

Buzzard Soaring

So long grounded

in himself, under such
feather weight

he seems to rise
out of a sack.

A dead poundage
re-assembles on the wings

spread into a sycamore key
turning. Earth breathes him out,

exhales him from his vantage,
to glide with the traffic between worlds,

the exploding galaxies of spores,
the seeds suspended in their shrouds.

The equality, the lightness here . . .
He feels his shadow separate

and travel the air, another
wanderer, another dust.

Below, history fires its
intricate acreage. Demesnes melt.

Towns bleed across ploughland.
Motorways grub like glaciers.

He suns. He sleepwalks on the wing
through this world and the next,

hearing the hormones hiss, hearing
the froth in his cells: *Re-enter*

the inferno. Rise again as ash.

Four Windows

One window looks over the ground
this cottage used to rent,
the thin strips across the river
they ditched and drained,
winter floodplain
where the yearlings summered:
now the plats have gone back
and the marsh climbs the hill.

One window looks over the road
to the stalls and shippons,
five sheds in a quarter acre:
haphazard joinery,
higgler's pigsties;
a carved pew-end hangs as a door,
latched with a nail; working silence,
whose uses lack their second hand.

One window looks to the hill slopes,
to the smooth sheep runs: half the year
a weather eye is all they need.
No half measures would work this land
that needs thrift and dry weather to
come together,
or dead growth and damp scorches it:
now below the contour
disuse is a slow fire.

One window looks back to my desk
– thriftless trade, whose measures
take time-and-a-half to complete.
One tune only answers
either master,
that ditch and line run clear, and sing.
I set my scale, work to this ground,
who can work it no other way.

Blue

Memory on a peg
behind the door:

the slip-leash a live line
through my fingers

that floats on his shoulders'
running water

or knows their stiffening
the undertow

of another presence
in the hedgebank

still rancorous with fox.
Always that shock

as the hackles rise on
a waking dream,

an ancient line stands out
in the young dog.

Slip him, and I become
the outer ear,

the iris of his eye,
ready to shout

if he conjures a fox
as he stag-leaps

and salmons the long grass.
Enter the land

within the land, a light
and shadow land

whose denizens are quick
and changing shapes,

where the pheasant's wing spreads
into dead wood,

and riddles of brown earth
in the stubble

or clods of bleached-out grass
in the furrow

soon as our backs are turned
go haring off.

Enter the light and dark
of the duel,

the dog's dive and dolphin
over the ground,

a shoulder gleam breaking
the air's surface,

a slate gleam, night closing
with each new stride,

the hare's running rings, her
lucky numbers,

noughts and figures of eight,
a breathing space

won on every turn.
Enter the dark

of that other duel
he fought, the leash

an allegiance he held,
a last life line.

Sorrow still rives me that
I let him slip.

Crows in Snow

Absences of motion, of colour.

Meteorite or moraine, black stones
half-in or half-out of the snow.

Only purpose survives

and has them belly down, black cones
of heat-absorption, solar cells

recharging in the sun

as if all has to be done again,
the ground to disclose its strata,

the minerals their millennia,

the fossil slates of Langenaltheim
split a second time, and flight feathers

print once, twice on the snow.

Gardening in Avernus

Evening in the turned earth.
A night wind foxes the grass.
Still, through the late afternoon
of stone, the thin scent rises
of a herb patch by the wall
and I am on a path of
that other garden, where thyme
is grey bush beyond the vines,
reptile over the dry rocks.

Cicadas stir the leaf fall.
The lych-owl pronounces dusk
over shadowless cedars.
The foraging pipistrelles
enter meridian blue.
A common scent of earth is
the black ship across Ocean,
a coast of willows and mist.
Without a trench of dark blood

I have come where the tenses
elide. The past re-opens
to a nervous link through an
electronic gate, or the
Gate of Horn. Cell by single cell
an identity wakes,
as over featureless distances
the sightlines form of
particular earth and hours.

Three stanzas in memoriam W.H. Auden

Draw back the sackcloth from the windows.
Lock the revolver in the desk drawer.
Another kind of silence
is entering at the open door.
In the writing lamp's circumference,
within the ambient dust,
a concentration is lost.

Throw the dust sheets over the Cave of Making.
Pile the thirteen volumes of the dictionary
alphabetically upon the floor.
Archaism returns to the antiquary,
logodaedaly to the admen and the law.
The leaves are silent. These oracles are dumb,
and history all that mystery can become.

Send Caliban back to Roy Plomley.
Call Ariel down from the shrouds.
Storm and sweet airs dissolve together
as that man with the hanging look simply
vanishes into the crowd.
All that it could take the magic took.
His staff lies broken: undrowned, his book.

Rosehill

i.

Cumulus forms and drifts.

                       Some
part of the children who play
here is light chasing on
an empty playground.

            Their voices
as they rise have distance in.

        On the edge of
the moving city they look over
the houses their grandparents
called *mushroom growth*.

ii.

History fell behind us,
in a crook of the river,
on another, lower hill,

a groundwork that goes down ten
centuries, or seven feet.

Two miles west, on a gravel terrace,
our speech is as a strong city:

in three names three gates still stand,
though the Southgate has fallen

– our security that the names come
unbidden, from time out of mind.

Here weather is the change a
shadow makes in the shape of
a wall, and the hours a depth
in the colour of the stone,

a past that we commute to,
old centres only the banks
can afford.

Bus queues line the Cornmarket,
bound for the outer estates.

The fare stage is in Old French.

iii.

Pitched into fields, on hillsides
where the postwar tide left them,
before the next high water,

seven prefabs are still here
to recall our origins.

The hill's first settlement. We
walk to the shops at the Top.
We wait at the roundabout
where the bus turns.

Change become stationary.
Silence made to be broken.

iv.

There is no way to know us.

An ungenerous culture,
nothing of our life appears.

Over eighty thousand years
what changes?
The caves come outside the rock,

the housebacks terrace the hill
under the terraces of
travelling cloud.

There is no way to know us,
except as we know ourselves,

involuntarily,
in the silences the old

still call *an angel passing,*
in the skin tremor they say is

someone walking on my grave,

or in an *eye* we call *the mind's*
opening, in children looking down

to their homes foreshortened at their feet.

Cloud darkens. The rain moves in,
and the hill is lit windows,
riding lights.

                The streets below
are shoreline houses, still points
beside an estuary.

v.

Winter sunlight defines us,
momentary hill figures,
in negative on lit slopes:

we are a footstep's shadow;
we are the echo of light.

As you turn to me, and in
turning take my arm,

the sun travels through our coats
to form unwoven matter
on fibres of light

and here
this slight and linear dark
where your shadow and mine cross.

Winter heat in the pavement;
a pigeon suns on a roof;

and for half or a minute
we are as old as the light.

The Broken Road

Water on the fields
sedged with white grass

Tarmac over flints
the flints wearing through

Walking again
along the broken road:

is it the road bears us up
or the brokenness?

As the upper sky darkens
a depth enters the pools,
corn gold suffuses the grass

The stones grow luminous as they dim

Out of the blue-blacks of the tar
the blues effloresce

Light is a bloom
a pollen of blue

It powders up under our feet

Culvert

Stone stepping over,
cushioning arch
of cut and canted
stones, road's instep
riding the dip

of older workings
with the grain of the rock,
weatherings underground,
where water tells
another story

at cross-purposes
to this: bright threads
under memory, that pool
in memory's loss. Here
is a Roman thread,

a forethought of stone.

Rites of Passage

*to Anthony Conran, in the year of his marriage,
the birth of his first child, and his father's death.*

Comfortable words, framed
in darker times than ours,
are ruined archways,

rusted gates, lych gate
or kissing gate, beaten paths
to love or death

that dwindle out of use.
As our forefathers knew,
their ways are grass

– a by-way their sense of
comfortable, a castle stump
in the marches

that marks where a language
lost its fight. The formless
is given ground.

A name thumbed from the map
wears a way back to
the capital.

Death blues a nail, and
climbs the ring finger
to the heart.

We are raided by
the inarticulate. Be *sober,
be vigilant,*

the Apostle says – watchwords since
requisitioned by General Booth
and Captain Lynch

while *our adversary* . . .
as a roaring lion is
all but extinct.

The last enemy is
amnesia. The synapses
lapse in the mind,

the keystones fall to the grass.
Roadmenders are few, roadmakers
almost none. All

but lost to philology
the adjective's active
ability

to say *comfort* where there is
nothing to be said, at *Brig o' Dread*
to find foothold.

! r before this other, this
excellent mystery, to give good luck
at the threshold.

The language is at a loss:
uncomfortable, unaccustomed
and unversed.

'Now cool it!' – honeyed voices
over the rasp of Jeremiah
grinding his axe –

'Adam has transplanted the Garden.
Time is becoming habitable
for the first time.

Ask the dead. They'd be here tomorrow
with *"We should have your problems!"*
And so they would.

They'd have the transplanted Garden
in one perpetual season,
stationary

in an arrested prime: every
floret held back to a *floruit*,
a moment's grace

or else . . . the disgrace,
the fade, the dissolve into
incoherence.

What would they say, the stone-
breaking dead, who broke the unspoken
into metal,

links of an embanked and culverted
spine, a strait road that stretched
to meet their god?

Death is the way we live. In time
the myth comes, and gathers us
to our long home.

Only ours is comfortless:
the consuming young; obsolescence
built-into the old.

Can we match our forefathers' active
speech, that *made* a good marriage
or a good death,

from the passive registry
the language has become, the syllables'
expanding files

of *developmental life crises*
or *maladaptive conflict
situations?*

While the elderly subscribe
to *Death Education*, a course in
creative dying.

A feather print in the rock,
psychosis is all we keep
of the *psyche*,

the brush of a fossil wing.

Homage to James K. Baxter

Despair is the only gift;
When it is shared, it becomes a different thing.

James K. Baxter: 'Letter from the Mountains'

A newsagent taking in the first papers
would see us taking shape at the counter,
the ghost trade, come for Mars and Old Holborn, sugar and smoke.

Each morning, a shortchanging of the shadows,
as they rose from areas and stairwells,
sleepless from skinpopping methedrine.

Ah! the nights on the road
on a mattress, 'on the move' through
the bleak indoors. Joe Tex sang of

stogies as we rolled our Social Security
into straights, played *Indianapoly* through the small hours:
the speed kings, firing on half an amp.

And yet it was almost good, to be one
of a tacit company, to be men without women,
low lifeforms in a basement room.

Only a few of us became serious ghosts.
Our selves shadowed us. Only the present
can be lost in Lethe,

as I would lose it now, for your company.
But the light breaks. And already the shapes
are forming at the counter.

Waiting for the Day

Plimsoles takes the floor. Blossoms as the Bar
whoops and whistles. As if he were
treading water, as if rough music were the water
where a strange nature uncurls and flowers,
he slow-motions to the door. Already in replay,
an old clip run and re-run, his white hipsters
step and flare. His white raincoat
capes and swirls. He is all woman.
We are all eyes.

Sullen, in black, his fetch
steps tersely at his side.

Shanghai? Marseilles? Tilbury.
Last light over warehouse roofs.
Darkness asphalts the waste ground.

Not a sound when he re-enters.
Buys an armful of beer cans. Outside,
hurls them one by one against the wall,

repeatedly. Gathers them up, shoulders
hunched in the white T-shirt.
Cradles them back to the ship.

We nurse our halves. Tomorrow
if a crew is short – someone
fails to report – one of us
will get a ship. On completion
of the trip, union papers.

Buzzards
for Ted Hughes

Hook beak, hawk wings and cross-hatchings
are old service patches

on battledressed veterans, who pudder
on their allotments of air.

Except the insignia will not fade.
Only the old soldiery never dies.

They have only to lift over the skyline
and the rook flak rises.

Each morning their mobbed shapes come
mewing from the wood, silhouettes of

a fear without armistice,
feather of a bad dream.

All afternoon they crest the telegraph poles,
the Third Reich in moult,

waiting for the earthworms to emerge,
waiting for the roads to deliver their dead.

In Transit

i. THE YOUNG SOLDIERS

Two weeks each of them has been away from home,
having a man made of him. In the legend
of small brothers. Behind reminiscence
in the Public Bar. And two days a figure
home on leave. Arms linked, the girls in the Disco
cross the floor in threes: hello, they say, stranger.

Strange to be anyone, invisibility
at the back of the class retained them so long.
Strange as their exchange of nowhere for nowhere,
out of work on the streets of Bolton and Colne
or well-paid patrolling the streets of Belfast.
They talk vaguely of a tour in Germany.

They think over and over of coming out
with a trade. The train removes them south once more
for combat training. Now they are drinking like
troopers; and it could be because they're half-cut
they're telling you this, their hands shake and they are
crying. In the same breath keeled over asleep.

ii. THE WEAPONS INSTRUCTOR

And even the experience he did not choose
is of no use.
                    In his mind as the train moves north
the hare's scream the boy gave as he jigged and shuddered,
cramped over the trigger.
                              'The Powers That Be, in their
wisdom . . .': an officer's way of saying he was refused
an engineering course, ten years ago. Since when
he has served the Powers in their wisdom,
sergeant to the raw generations, technical
specialist into an old sweat of thirty three.

'Well, keep an eye on him, Sergeant.' As if
he hadn't. As if he had spoken out of turn.

Course continues. He continues to keep an eye.
Course ends with the new rifle, for use in Ulster.
Which all the recruits always take seriously.
Which this one takes in rigid hands.
                                        And at once fires,
a spasm of rapid fire in which he reels and screams,
still firing.
            One man killed. Two of them all their strength
to get the gun off him/release him from the gun.

Manslaughter. And the hare's scream of the slaughterer.
A hare's brain of fear.
                    Put it all down to
experience. Wisdom is for the officers.

iii. THE PROFESSIONALS

Stout McGuinness and *Twomey's Flit* fill the carriage,
cassettes of jigs and reels, recorded off-duty
in pubs, in front rooms after hours – and over here
not quite the thing, as glances from the businessmen
imply. Have they gone native? The usual Yahoos.

Such is emergency, this side of the water.
A motley of khakis, camouflage and civvies,
a shambles of boots and shoes: soldiers returning
in the privilege of action, all-licensed by
sheer relief; who none the less turn down their cassettes,

being, more than anything, tired. And settle themselves.
Close down. The hours are absorbed into their posture,
one with the hours of the nights of their tour, the days
of years they have traded in for a trade, a skilled
future. Lloyds would not insure their education:

but the roster will see them back over the water,
from exercises off Cyprus with the Sixth Fleet,
manoeuvres on Aldershot or Luneberg Heath,
to the narrow, boarded streets where they have become
more or less at home among those who resent them.

The Doppel Gang

OR BETTER BY HALF, WHEREIN THE HASIDIC PRINCIPLE
IS APPLIED TO HISTORY.
*Others, to restore the balance, claim that . . . there were actually two Baal
Shem Tovs and that the Hasidic movement was founded . . . by the other.*

Elie Wiesel: *Souls on Fire*

His sonatas will end up as curl papers; his landlady use his symphony
for lining a trunk; several execrable Irish ballads live on. As a violinist
he barely, as they say, scrapes a living. Of late, the further to fiddle his
creditors, has followed the Armies to Brussels, where he has earned
the sobriquet of *Maréchal Nez*. There was a time his looks brought him
heirs and disgraces. Now the wits ask if he bows with his nose. The
Beau Monde is thick with wits. No matter. Five francs are not to be
sneezed at. Another set forms up on the floor. He shakes himself: 'Stop
woolgatherin', Wellesley.' Up strikes the music. And there he is again,
a stooped, unmilitary shadow, second fiddle at the Duchess of Rich-
mond's Ball, on the eve of Waterloo.

Litter blows over the Park. The length and breadth of the Crystal
Palace, the sunlight exhibits the dust. Hobnails grind between the
aisles. Knuckles rap, sizing up the wood of the stands. Hereon had
men glimpsed a City. The New Jerusalem, with working models. With
the last word in Progress, the Alpha and Omega: universal suffrage
and sewerage. But here comes the universal appliance, a man in his five
wits. Why, it's Albert Francis Charles Augustus Emanuel. And look-
ing quite the everyday article, in moleskin trousers, flannel shirt and a
stud. Not, it seems, the gentleman from Saxe-Coburg-Gotha. But from
the German colony in Manchester. Demolition contractor to the Great
Exhibition. He shoulders a length of heart of oak. 'Long as there's one
to set it up,' he winks, 't'other 'll clear it away.'

Outside, the sirocco. Inside, as cool as a catamite's fingertip. The
houseboys, the Arab, the Italian, and the Swede, are deep in Monopoly.
Foundation Studies. They plan to be sleek and sixty, rich gourmands
of little delicacies. Like *milord*, who has just switched off the wireless.
Really, if it wasn't that it so worried the Vichy, he would throw the
thing away. All that guff *On the Beaches*. That antiphonal fuss over
The Few. And now, believe it or not, *Their Finest Hour*. That the lan-
guage should be so harrowed! Spencer is quite disgusted with Winston.
He dispatches a winged word: 'You know, duckie, I sometimes wonder
which of us is camp.'

The Hooded Gods

three male gods of healing, fertility, and the underworld.
from a stone plaque in Housesteads Museum, Hadrian's Wall.

These are the odds and sods among the gods,
the other ranks, the omnipresences,
teamen, charmen, male midwives: the daily helps
from history's basement, the caretakers

who rarely come to light. They have become
their deliverances, their many hands
beneath notice and now beyond telling.
They surface from the sleep of history

whose care suffuses history like sleep,
powers of recovery and repair
who keep the middle watch, the graveyard shift,
the seamsters who knit up the ravelled sleeve.

Empire succeeds empire over their heads.
The paces centuries set in the Wall
have doubled under artillery wheels.
Now low-flying Phantoms ghost from the stones.

Their histories are the interleaves,
the pages happiness has written white.
They show as lapses in the chronicle,
or specks of dialect in letters home.

No stars in their eyes. No shrinking either.
These are the hard core. These are the heart's wood.
Three grey bottles still standing on the Wall.
Three pollards who can make a fist of green.

The Night Self

Fin nos, wrth fwrw lludded.

Now the puckish humours leave your face.
The skin acknowledges the bone.
The presence is as one
of the individual and the race.
In motherhood you will not look so strong,
nor in death so young.

Lower Lumb Mill

*for Ellie; and for the teachers and pupils of Nicholls Ardwick
School, Manchester, who spent a week writing at Lumb Bank.*

i.

Here are the reins of
the work horse, the traces
of water in harness,

still handstitched in stone:
and not slack, though water
falls in idleness, though weather

buffs and beeches the black
of the chimney that once blackened
the beeches; and still rises

out of all proportion
to rocks and stones and trees,
a first draught, a delineation

of valleys since transfigured
by cubes and planes and cones,
a shadow of Hell or Halifax,

45

of mills and manufactories
wherever water ran,
terracings and resurfacings

worn through again as the work
moves away. Now tree shadows
box the walls. Green thoughts

wash at the drystone. Or,
under the petrodollar's
green shade, green thoughts

walk down from Lumb Bank. Between
anorak and wellingtons, jay's
wingflashes of tight sateen

as the walking disco, Angela,
Jennifer, Beverley and Mo,
sends a green blue beat through

the thoughtful thrush-tap on stone
of the geologist's hammer
Mohammed would like to have,

and stirs Farah's tree of silence,
just broken into the first leaf
of her sketchbook. Our other lives

star the valley, the Persephone
in each of us given five days
above ground. Half-thoughts, slim chances,

huddle at the valley's rim,
wind-silvered underleaves,
the ghosts of our fits and starts.

'Where to go from here?'
A rainflash of fieldfares turns
into dust shaken from a duster.

Out of memory a ring-dove calls,
Darby, be true, Darby . . .
And truly, where can we go?

ii.

Even as we ask, a road
finds our feet. Gently down,
under moss'd tree roots,

between banks of primroses.
Sunlight mullioned through branches.
Madrigals of blackbird and thrush.

Now the hill is a honeycomb
of lanes we wander two by two,
in conspiracies of reverence,

little arches of whispering heads.
Each couple through its kissing gate
threads onto a village green

the generations in their loveknots
have stitched as white as the may.
Here is a month of Sundays.

Afternoon is a tune
from Elgar, on which the sun,
in a setting by Vaughan-Williams,

never sets. Elms constable
the high clouds. Yews cloister
the path. The lawns are mown

to a Regency stripe. We walk
under great protections,
into wise enclosures.

Distantly, distinctly,
as clear as the voice of Clare,
a yellowhammer sings,

*A little bit of bread
and no cheese. A little bit
of bread and no cheese.*

The lawns spin like roulette wheels.
Cloud smokes in a ring. Towers of
coin rise on fields of baize.

The Trade Winds blow us back
to our places. Beverley? Mo?
Unheard of. Battened under hatches

Bristol fashion. Ship's ballast
to the Indies, or King
Cotton's fields. Mohammed?

Locked in a Kipling ballad
– one of many who move
between the lines, and serve

the twenty six soldiers
of lead, appearing only
as points of silence.

As for me, who should I be
but Hodge? The original blot
on the landscape, the labourer

beyond the ha-ha, who trespasses
twice a year on the park
of English poetry, the blackface

morrising and mumming
through the gates. Clodhopper.
Clown. Brother to the ox.

iii.

Now *Teacher! Teacher!* pages me
through the wood. Wordsworth sermons
in stones. Tennyson riffles

in the brook. Those two metallic
tones pulse. Siren song. Nerve
twitch. Quartz chimes on my wrist.

Hard to learn my own lesson:
to listen as voices rise
on other paths, to look up

into the star haze of buds
and see the twigs jigsaw
and piece the light. One step

up the slope, at eye level,
a beech sapling breaks
into a galaxy. Two arcs

swirl out, encircling
a space the buds orbit
in planetary calm.

How they keep station and
constellation, equidistant
in the wind-flattened flame!

Last night, all at sea
in the surge of the bluebeat,
a white face in the trough

of a wave, I trod water
and watched you drown
one step away. Then someone

took a hand. We circled
and centred in a star.
The star flowered and flowed

back into bud, we swung out
and danced in, our hands linked
and rising to a crest,

rising to gull shrieks and skirls,
triumph and delight and hope and fear,
one wave of the earth.

This morning was full tide,
a mirror of quiet. We were deep
in our reflections. We mused

into coffee mugs. Toasted marshmallows
on the fire. The hearth held us
in its gravity. I watched you

as you sat in the sofa corner
listening to Sue. Listening
is your trance. I shall always see you

poised over the ashtray
on your knee. You lean back
on your elbow to inhale,

you lift your face. Eyes closed,
you dream a moment, Delphic
in the haze. This morning

was different. You leaned forward,
listening head and shoulders
to Sue. Whose life was it?

Who was listening in you?
You were rigid with recall.
I glimpsed you at fifteen,

the family manager:
your father in and out of work,
a man of hopeless charm,

your mother in the damp flat,
bright-eyed on barbiturates;
and you the ghost of a child

50

grown-up half-grown, mothering
and motherless. How we are hurt
into being! Made and marred

in the same breath. To watch you
kindling in a smile, immediate,
healing, acute, is to watch you

give yourself away.

iv.

And so I come
to the valley's head, where the path
turns towards home. *Come out!*

Come out! sweetly reasons
a song thrush, *Over the moor
lies The New Delight.* And I think

of all the streets we have paced,
all our unseeing circuits
of the park. Each despair.

Each renewal. Of whole families
who war in us. Each mother
and father of a row. 'Stop being

so bloody English!' you once shot
at my verray parfit gentil knyght.
And down I came off my high horse.

My love, how would you disarm us now?
Of our hurts? Our history?
Unhappiness is a ghetto

– we turn in blind alleys
where words have their own quarrels
and a touch ends in a shrug.

If I could catch what is baffled
and battles in us, negotiates
and is unnegotiable . . .

I think of Jennifer, farmed out
to her grandmother in Barbados,
bringing home all she has to bring:

her difference, her awkward truth.
And then of Sue, meeting her mother
outside the cinema once a week.

They buy their popcorn and hardly speak.
It's early days. But as the lights dim
they sit together. Their faces lift.

They are looking out of next Friday
in Ardwick. Mo bites her lip
on the check-out, her eyes down

under the queue of eyes: 'they watch
as each item is put through: they know
your mistakes even before you do.'

While in the corner shop, tin
by tin, Mohammed takes stock
of his mother's English. Then sighs

and begins again. Concentrations
of work and love, mirrored
in the plate glass of the malls,

multiplied in the windows
of the estates; and still locked
into this valley's stone setts

and revetments, the work surface
that is all we inherit
of the earth; the wheel-shaft

deep as a canal lock; the dye-pits
that square-off these upper slopes;
the waggon-road's steady gradient

my feet already incline to
as second nature. *Come out!*
Come out! insists the song thrush

and a wind shivers the ferns
on the bank. Remember how
as lovers we moved from sign

to sign? How two magpies glided
the length of our path? Goldfinches
glinted from hedge to hedge

braiding our walk? Every day
brought its confirmation,
its laying-on of wings.

Now I watch the full moon
of your forehead – *swan's breast*,
the bards would have sung, *blossom*

of the heaven bough – cloud over
and your shoulders 'conform
to the yoke', you once wrote,

a slight, preoccupied stoop,
and my arms reach out in tenderness,
blind tenderness, to hold you

and renew the harm. At this point
there is no sign. Only the road's
grits and micas, the scuffed shine

that could prove another circuit
of hell, or the last mile
we must go, though it strip us

to the bare bone.

Skara Brae
for Frances and Adam

The dunes of peat ash,
the skears of scraped-out shells,
the gravel of animal bones, the flocks of sand,

all worked to a hard mothering,
a weathertight skin of clay
hummocked over the huts: embryos

in chamber tombs, mound dwellers
under their own midden, they pressed
out of the vortex engraved on their pots,

childbearing children, dead at twenty;
learned to bait bone splinters with limpets
softened in freshwater; to twist heather

into simmons tethering the stock; to staunch bleeding
with the puff-ball's black gauze; step by step
moved away from the swallow-hole.

In fine weather they broke surface. Knappings
and food scraps littered the roof of the mound.
Here are the good days, the hours in the sun.

Water rose as they bent to the spring,
the ram's horn of water rose for them,
and they saw themselves as water's face,

as luck's two hands, fastening sheepskin
with a bone pin, polishing oxhide
with an ox knuckle. They scoured

Note: Skara Brae is a Stone Age village in the sand dunes of
Orkney, covered over by a great storm in prehistoric times and
uncovered by another storm in the last century. 'Skear' is
northern dialect for a mussel scar, an off-shore ridge or
sandbank exposed at low tide.

the sea's scourings: soft horns of driftwood
that were American spruce; dry foam of pumice
from Icelandic lava flows. Worked on their luck,

grinding a gannet's bone into the pumice
until it was sharp enough for an awl,
hollowing an antler until it held an axehead.

Bored through cattle teeth. Bored through a walrus tusk.
Out of salvage and scrap built up a bead hoard,
a string of good days. Began to bank on their luck.

Set spy-holes into passages valved with stone slabs,
secreted it in treasure cells. Until the mound was
another mouth on the foreshore, swallowing all it could use.

Hunger is stilled now. Now there is only stillness:
the hearth swept; the quernstone at rest in the quern,
in the churn-hole of rock, a fossil of water in spate.

Here is the life they hardly knew, the quiet enshrined
on the shelves of their stone dresser, or glimpsed
out to sea, the horizon's back shelf of light

still clear and still out of reach: a persistence
of charms and undergleams, of secrecies and stowings,
a necklace tucked into the heather of the boxbed

or spilled over the threshold. White dribbles down,
the gutted fish leaking its roe, the skinned hare
her milk under the skin. All their luck let slip

at the last, the string snapped on the narrow door
they scrambled through, as the wind darkened
and the dunes began to run like the sea.

At Vanishing Point
para Eugenia en El Cántaro

This morning we talk again
under the bony plum,

whose fruit, like a stone
sucked in the mouth,

can outwit thirst. I sit
on the garden seat as on

the bench of the ship of souls,
lashed to my oar. Almost hear,

between the tick-birds and
the parakeets, a gull's keen,

invoking solitude, the doom
of the Seafarer, who dreams

of a hearth and companions, and wakes
to the ice of the whale-road.

My salve for hard times
is to make them harder still.

You do that too. You will
when I leave. Lock yourself

in your painter's attic
in Bogotá. Work to

the wry songs of Bola de Nieve.
Geni, you and I are two

of a kind. I find you
on the bench beside me.

Above us, like a daydream, like a thought
moored between two pillars of cloud,

El Cántaro, the house you built
out of stubbornness, out of shipwreck.

It is just pencilled in
against the sky. Just held

at the point of erasure.
Built of shadings, cross-hatchings,

a pencil sharpening the whiteness
of paper, constructing

a moebius strip of light,
endless galleries, rising

scales of roof, ascending
and descending stairs.

The pencil sketched, suffered
erasure, sketched again.

One by one the variants
emerged. Plumped onto the page

and sank without trace. Stepped out
on their spindleshanks

and crumpled into the pits
of erasure, the hubbub of forms

jostling for life. Then the pencil
took wing. Took from the swift's wing

the long, honed line, that austere
primary glide. Took from the owl's wing

the crossing of tenons, that secondary
softness of flight. Something lifted

that could fly. Now we live under its wing.
Watch the diamond lattice compose the light

and the stairs rise in counterpoint. Hear
the three-part harmony in the turn of the stair.

Geni, we came here already erased.
All that life we lived on paper,

all the ways and means we had sketched
in our letters. What precise negations,

what scar-white lines your ghost must have crossed
to find me. I was a blankness walking

on the white fires of that grid.
Now we talk. My fingers touch the blade

of your shoulder. And are fingers
on warm skin. We touch as only survivors

can touch. Butterflies like blue water
lap the air. The charcoal tree has blossomed

into featherdusters of flame. We could walk down
to the Sumapaz, the Peaceable River,

naming the white humped cattle, the hawk
who is a call, a circling

shadowed by her young, the lizards
who are known only by their vanishing.

The Roof Tree
for Bibiana in Ladywell

Coming to call you for supper,
I enter a visible hush,
the cat's cradle of reflections
your writing lamp throws on the wall.
No more than glances off whitewash,
three or four spills of light, it seems
to open a luminous depth
of projections and precisions.
One triangle slants its clear field
across another's ridge of light,
as if the stars were focused there,
their constancies, their still waters
crystallised in a quartz of light.

A hand's breadth of transparency,
it forms above your head, one of
the stations I make in passing,
a scallop shell of quiet – and
would vanish if I came closer,
a silence in your own language
that is sounding the dry water
of these stones. I pause in the door,
afraid to break the first hair's breadths
of belonging, threads and sensings
that are making of this spare room
a familiar solitude,
a separateness that is home.

Downstairs your sister sits cross-legged
in the stereo's cockpit glow,
her body earthed and her headphones
filtering the empyrean
as a baroque trumpet ascends
through the firmament, its pinpoint
of angels feathering the blue.
While your mother sips her whisky
in front of a makeshift easel
– the stepladder with two nails in –
and contemplates these zinc yellows,

fragile, underwater yellows
whose phosphorus burns in water.

My notebook is open: but for once
it's enough to be house and home,
to set bowls on the low table
and wait. The stillnesses still hold,
each separate stillness that shelves
beneath the archipelago
of lights. The house rides on silence.
And though the evening ahead
has an old magic, renewing
our ring of faces in firelight,
I would rather keep the quiet
of the lamps in their far reaches,
the depth of stars under the roof.

The clovers in the salt-glazed jar
– one find in another's keeping –
raise their hussar heads and brisk out
their purple busbies. And I steel
every nerve for your going.
Intimate and homely, like breaths
drawn in sleep, the silences stir
and sigh. Catches and quickenings.
Easings and settlings. A massive,
multitudinous calm, as though
the roof tree had branched and blossomed,
a chestnut setting a candle
in every window of leaf.

From the Pampas
Four Native American poems
translated from Spanish versions

1 PRAYER TO THE SUN

Give me my blue sky for ever,
ancient man with the lit face.
Give me my white cloud over and over,
old soul with the fiery head.
Give me your golden shelter for ever,
great knife of gold in whose gleam
we stand here on earth.

2 OUR PRAIRIE

This, brothers, is our wide earth
where nothing stays, everything goes,
the wind restless, the horizon always on the move.

This, brothers, is our broad earth.
We make camp. When the weather shifts,
we shift camp. This is how we live.

This, brothers, is our pampas.
It's not narrow ground. It's good and broad.
Room for everyone, all the room you want.

3 MY FRIEND, BROTHER WIND

I have travelled the land, my friend.
I know where I have been, my friend.
Truvolusicó: know it well,
I was over that way, my friend.
Urrelaquén: know it well,
I was over that way, my friend.
Napoleofú: know it well,
I was over that way, my friend.
Acamahuida: know it well,

61

I was over that way, my friend.
My friend, brother wind,
I have been everywhere.
I know where I have been,
My friend, brother wind.

4 SONG OF THE LAND

My land,
Don't go away from me,
Don't be missing from me,
However far away I go.

Death Song
Quechua poem from Peru
translated from a Spanish version

Wake up, woman.
Get up, woman.
There is a dog howling
in the middle of the street.

Death is coming,
the dancers are coming.

When the dancers come,
you have to join on the end.
When death comes,
that's it, my friend.

El Día del Amor

Driving along la Séptima, the main road into the centre of Bogotá, we find ourselves blocked by a high-speed convoy. Two Toyota Land Cruisers are shepherding a black Mercedes. One hugs its back bumper. The other sways beside it in the outside lane. Then we glimpse the roof of a third in front. The back door of the rear Toyota is wavering, as if it's about to fly open. I can see a hand gripping the window-frame and I am expecting it to open the door and slam it properly shut. Until the door swings out on a bend and I see the neat black muzzle of a sub-machine-gun. The hand pulls the door to, as a woman might slip a bra strap back under her dress, but holds it ajar, ready to fling it open the moment the Mercedes is blocked. I think of one of the children's drawings *Semana* printed yesterday in an article on the psychological effects of the violence. Underneath the child had written: 'We're really afraid of the bodyguards. They're so edgy and they leap out of their cars and fire without thinking of the school buses going past with children in.'

Eugenia, meanwhile, is curious to see who's in the black Mercedes. She accelerates past the rear Toyota. This seems to me a little unwise but we're running into traffic now and the convoy itself accelerates, dodging left and right wherever there's a gap, and swerving back into formation. The rear-gunner is ahead of us again, the back door veering open and the little black snake's tongue of the gun barrel flickering in and out. But no one's niftier than Eugenia in the hurtle and lurch of Bogotá traffic. As the convoy bears off to the right, she slips up on the inside. Someone we don't recognize, a man in his sixties with a bald spot in thick brown hair, is leaning back on the cushions and talking to an elegant grey-haired woman beside him. With his right hand he is making a slow gesture, as if, in the course of a reflective Sunday afternoon drive, he were developing some subtle point.

There are no sodium lights in Bogotá. Street lighting is subdued and darkness presses down from the mountains, so thick you can almost rub it between your fingers.

Driving at night is like navigating between islands. You cross deep pools of tree shadow. The sunken lake of a park. Run across a strip of light – a shop-front, an office building – where the shadows are mobile. One leans out of a doorway. Another detaches itself from the angle of a wall. They are private security guards, a single-barrelled shotgun hung over their shoulder. Then trees swallow you again. The long canal of the central reservation. You pass a sentry-box at the entrance to a residential estate, a figure reading a newspaper in an oblong of light.

Every café and restaurant has its jetty, its strip of lit pavement. You pull in and an attendant comes to the edge. He motions you up to the kerb. He finds you a mooring. You almost expect him to throw you a rope.

These are the Fortunate Isles. Beyond lies the south of the city, an uncharted bayou where millions live in rudimentary houses, along unpaved roads.

Even those teeming alleys must be deserted now, the charcoal braziers of the roast corn-cob and kebab stalls smoking quietly into the night. Colombia's second city, Medellin, where the terrorists began, had thirty-seven bombs in a fortnight and was under curfew for three weeks. It took just one bomb to turn Bogotá into a ghost city after dark. That was the lorry bomb that cracked open the offices of *El Espectador* and covered the printing presses and the news desks in fallen plaster and broken glass. We live on the other side of the city but the rumble seemed to be right in our roof beams. At first, I thought the building's huge satellite dish, the size of a radio telescope, had collapsed.

Since then people have been taking no chances. By nine o'clock the streets are empty. Restaurants still open. Lamps burn on the quays. But the trees arch into the night, their dark masses unbroken. No flares of green from approaching headlights.

Last week a friend took us out to dinner. Entering the restaurant I felt like a coin clicking into the slot of a penny arcade. The waiters were standing between the empty tables with their arms folded. There was just one other couple, a pair of lovers at a corner table, locked into each other's gaze. Our penny dropped and the restaurant whirred into motion. The waiters crossed the floor. The barman clinked among his glasses. They took off the *boleros* and put on some *salsa*. But no one else dropped in and the machinery soon ran down. The waiters refolded their arms. The barman went back to his newspaper.

We sat by the window and looked down on to the still lights of the city. We were up on la Calera, the great ridge that rises to the north of Bogotá. A hundred feet of solid rock, I thought, between us and the road. Impossible to bomb.

The lovers were still there when we left. They had had a tiff, the man stiffening in his chair, the woman laughing and throwing her arms around his neck. Now she had him wound back into a close embrace. I saw their two cars, side by side in the car-park, and suddenly made the connection: it was the perfect time for an affair. They had the city to themselves.

I tend to gauge the level of tension by the number of soldiers in the next street. A Supreme Court judge lives there. Two years ago when I first came to Bogotá to join Eugenia for the summer, there were two soldiers outside day and night, guarding the building. Last year there were three. This year there are four.

They used to be very relaxed. I'd see one down at the phone box, ringing his girl-friend. Or borrowing the guitar from the man in the sweet stall and playing it with his sub-machine-gun slung across his back. Or I'd find one in front of me in the bakery. As we pressed towards the counter, the gun became like a shoulder-bag or an umbrella, one of those hard edges you mould yourself round in a queue. Its stubby snout nudged familiarly against my chest.

Now they are always along the kerb, checking on anyone who tries to park outside the building, or in front of the bank opposite. Car bombs are the latest weapon and suddenly everyone is vulnerable: the man in the black Mercedes because bodyguards are irrelevant and no one is quite sure whether a bullet-proof car can be made bomb-proof; and the rest of us because car bombs are indiscriminate. In May a car bomb on la Séptima just missed General Maza Márquez, the head of the Security Service, as a four-car convoy swept him to the office. Just missed because the terrorist was a fraction of a second late on the remote control and a passing Renault took the force of the blast. The General's bullet-proof car was wrecked and the convoy scattered across the road. But the real casualties were among the passers-by: a woman on the bus to work; a policeman walking home off the night shift; a little girl standing on the kerb, waiting for a school bus; and the man in the Renault, who just happened to be the father of an ex-Minister.

Every time we drive home, the one-way system takes us past the small skyscraper where the judge has his flat. Iron gates are drawn across the forecourt. The porter's lodge has dark, bullet-proof windows. At night it looks even more sinister. The light from the lodge catches on the soldiers' helmets, on the fluorescent No Parking sign they move out into the road. The first time we saw them, we stopped and reversed out of the street.

By day, Bogotá's street life washes back in, the sellers of anything and everything, *salsa* on their portable radios, their street cries amplified through little hand-held loudspeakers, *¡Lavadoras!, ¡Aspiradoras!* Washing Machines Repaired! Vacuum Cleaners!, a constant, irrepressible commerce. Twenty yards from their high-security zone, the soldiers have allowed two lads to set up a car washing service. In this select street, tacked on to a telegraph pole, has appeared a split end of wood, a bit of broken plank or an old fencing slat, announcing in uneven white paint: wE wAsh aNd sHinE yOur caR. Trade doesn't seem to be brisk but the lads have brought a radio and lie on the grass, flipping through tabloids. Someone has set up another sweet stall. Bank messengers in their smart suits stop, and buy gum, and gossip.

At times street life makes security impossible. Every red traffic-light announces a two-minute market. Vendors move between the lines of cars, selling newspapers, duty-free Marlboro's, the latest García Márquez. Others offer home-made biscuits and sweets: light, crisp *obleas*, like huge communion wafers filled with *arequipe*, a kind of condensed milk; rounds of real gelatine, boiled from cows' bones and sweetened with cane sugar. Black women from Choco carry trays of *alegrías* on their heads, balls of popcorn stuck together with cane sugar. Children sell the fruits of Colombia's twice-yearly summers: little leathery-skinned tropical plums that explode on your tongue in a starburst of sweetness; *pomarrosas* that would have delighted Oscar Wilde because biting into them is like biting into a wad of rose petals. And sometimes, as happened last week in Medellin, threading through all this come gunmen posing as cigarette sellers, who shoot a former mayor as he sits between his chauffeur and his bodyguard, waiting at the lights.

What is at stake is the character of a country which, for all its problems, has always been a pleasure to live in. The drug barons are exerting their subtlest, most persuasive pressure on just this point. Life will not be worth living, they are saying, if the government does not negotiate. The recent bombs have not been intended to cause casualties, which would further unite the country against them. Placed in banks, building societies, schools and supermarkets at night, when the buildings are empty, they are designed to cause panic, to make people ask themselves, 'Where will it all end?' Ironically, the more security measures the authorities impose, the more persuasive the blackmail becomes.

Threats can be almost as disruptive as bombs themselves. Calls have been made to schools and colleges, *el terrorismo telefónico*. Terrorists stole a van from the water company and toured Bogotá, broadcasting warnings that the supply had been contaminated. Poisoning on such a scale is actually almost impossible. Whole fleets of tankers would have to pump chemicals into the reservoirs, an operation that could hardly go unnoticed. But many people shut their water off. The authorities had to restore confidence by announcing that scientists were keeping a twenty-four hour watch, testing the supply every hour.

Another rumour was that *el Día del Amor y la Amistad*, a kind of extended Valentine's Day in which families, lovers and friends all exchange presents, would turn into *el Día de la Muerte*. They would assassinate Barco. They would blow up the Presidential Palace. There were many variants.

El Día is one of the fiestas where families gather and drink rum and *aguardiente* and dance through till dawn. South Americans do not leap about, thumping the ground with their feet, as Europeans and North Americans do. They dance from the ground upwards. Their feet softly paddle and their hips begin to sway. It's the release of a communal rhythm. Children wriggle like elvers in a spring tide. The old yield to it gravely, like trees to the wind. And the young dance as angels might make love, their hips close, fluent and inexhaustible, their feet hardly touching the ground.

This year it was a sad day. The authorities pulled out all the stops. They mobilized the cadets from the army and police colleges. They blocked all the roads into Bogotá and searched everyone entering the city. The police chief appeared on television, exhorting people to go out and enjoy themselves. But the discothèques on la Calera stayed empty. The dance-floors in the small towns were closed.   (1989)

Vivir Pobre

It's hard to imagine what under-development means until you have experienced it. Last year we had to queue on the road from Medellin to Barranquilla because a landslide had swept part of it away. The road, the only link between Colombia's main industrial city and its principal port, had been closed all weekend. Now it was open again, but only just. We sat in the Jeep, dwarfed by the huge *tractomulas* that haul Colombia's freight. Macks and Chevrolet Super Brigadiers, their cabs festooned with lights, their long bonnets carrying silhouettes of naked women on the radiator and a statue of the Virgin Mary on the air-filter. Three hours it took, inching forward through the rain, before we came to what they had managed to rebuild of the road: a single lorry's width of gravel and mud, shelving precariously on a steep hillside.

The usual vendors had appeared out of nowhere. They trudged along the line of lorries, offering peanuts roasted in cane sugar, bottles of *aguardiente*, cans of beer. One man had a big cardboard box of *saltinas*, salt biscuits. As he walked past us, the soggy cardboard finally

67

gave way and the packets of biscuits spilled out on to the verge. He was gathering them up, trying to hold the box together with plastic and string, when he saw us watching him. He looked up and gave a wry smile: *'Vivir pobre es muy sabroso, gracias a Dios.'* 'Thank God, the life of the poor has a flavour all of its own.' (1989)

Tierra Caliente

Friday evening. I walk through Melgar, taking in the different atmosphere of *tierra caliente*: the warm, earth smell of the streets, which refracts after rain into as many odours and scents as there are bands of colour in the wet pebbles; the whitewashed, windowless houses, sitting like cool cellars inside their thick mud walls; the succession of open front doors, each one like an old-fashioned radio, a panel of yellow light under a carved surround, sending dance music out into the street. A man in white shorts is sitting out on his chair. He pushes his heels down and rocks the chair back, stretching voluptuously, like a cat, in the middle of the street.

In Colombia, climate changes with altitude. On Friday afternoons, like many inhabitants of Bogotá, we drive to the edge of the high plateau on which the city stands. Mist hangs over the pines and eucalyptus as warm air from the valleys below condenses on the slopes. Swerving between the *tractomulas* and the manic buses of the *Expreso Bolivariano*, we drive helterskelter down the side of the Andes, dropping seven thousand feet in an hour and a half.

Helterskelter is the word. The road is one long fairground, lit by flashing neon signs and simple strings of yellow bulbs, lined with stalls selling the produce of each successive climate and cafés specialising in every conceivable local dish, from the thick soups of the highlands to the fish stews of the tropical rivers.

The *Sabana*, the high plateau, offers cheeses and fresh meat. A pig's head swings on a hook while its intestines, in the form of *morcillas* and *chorizos*, black puddings and spicy sausages, steam in the glass case below. Halfway down, at the height of the coffee plantations, the stalls hardly need their fringe of bulbs. They glow with fruit, banked fires of oranges under the bananas' hanging lamps, which taper in layer after layer like the beads on a chandelier. These are *manzanitos,* little bananas you can squeeze out of their skins and eat in one soft mouthful. Approaching Melgar and the long plain that grows Colombia's best rice, palm-thatched kiosks begin to sell coconuts, mangoes, papayas, and green clusters of *mamoncillos*, a dry, unpromising little rind, hardly bigger than an oak-apple. Crack it open in your mouth and it proves to be a lychee. (1991)

Living in Colombia

The response of the girl on Passport Control at Heathrow was typical. 'Where have you just come from, sir?' she asked as she took my passport. 'Bogotá,' I replied. 'Oh, Christ!' she said, and handed it straight back, as if it might still be charged with danger.

I have spent much of my time in Colombia over the last five years. Only once have I experienced anything like danger. It was during the Drug War, when a bomb went off in the next street. I had called at a friend's flat to collect an article of mine she had translated into Spanish. I was browsing along the book-lined walls, just thinking that I could immure myself there for days, when the noise of the blast came through them as if they were rice-paper. For a moment the world went into negative. Everything that had seemed substantial, so securely there, myself included, felt transparent. The only solid thing was that sound. A little closer, it said, and you and your friend and all her books would be shredded on the wind.

One evening I happened to see the Justice Minister coming home from work. Two police outriders came zipping up the street on their Yamahas, followed by the Minister's limousine, closely followed by a white Toyota Landcruiser. As the Minister's car slowed to turn into the block of flats where she lived, a whistle shrieked and the doors of the Toyota flew open. Bodyguards leapt out, their sub-machine-guns held up in the air, and ran with the limousine down into the underground car-park. Thirty seconds of drama on the other side of the street. Another thirty seconds and the traffic was flowing normally. The lights changed to red and the old cigarette-seller on the corner waved her pack of contraband Marlboros at the waiting cars.

Living in Colombia is like that. Danger is not ubiquitous. Nor, unless the drug barons mount a bombing campaign, is it indiscriminate. It has particular targets whom it keeps in its sights, shadowing them wherever they go. The rest of us just glimpse it occasionally, on the other side of the street. (1991)

Walking Off the Fear

EXTRACTS FROM THE JOURNAL OF A RESIDENCY

In 1992 I spent six months as Writer in Residence at the Blyth Valley Disabled Forum, working with housebound disabled people and their carers. I had some experience of what it meant to be a carer, having nursed my late wife, the poet Frances Horovitz, in the terminal stages of cancer. Frances and I had started our life together in the North East and to return there was to return to an area charged with strong memories.

These first few days are not easy. The promised council flat is not ready and I have to stay on at William Martin's house in Sunderland, just a few streets up from Thornhill Gardens, where Frances and I lived in our first eighteen months together.

Each morning I wake at four. Not a gradual awakening, the head a lit window in a still-darkened body. I come awake like a surfer on a board, all my faculties braced, already trying to balance on the great surge of energy that is hurtling me into the day.

I distrust this energy. Vitality, it says, I am vitality, and tries to join in the dawn chorus. But it sings too loud. Deep down I suspect it is fear.

All I can do is walk it off. When first light comes at five, I slip out of the house and walk down to Thornhill Park.

It is cold for the end of June. I button my donkey jacket up and pull the Orkney wool hat out of my pocket.

In Thornhill Park I squat against the trunk of a tree and listen to the wind. The energy comes in gusts. When it blows thin, I feel cold and tired. What I really want is breakfast. But I'm shut out of the house now and I'll have to stay out.

I drop down to the brook and follow it through the park, remembering how I used to exercise my lurchers here, throwing sticks across the brook they would leap tirelessly, back and forth.

Once I had Flash and three of her sons on the leash, such a draught of power from their slim fishbacks that I felt like Neptune in his chariot being pulled by dolphins.

The first time I let them all off together, they fanned out across the path with a menace so visible I never risked it again. They had turned into sharks – the Sharks from *West Side Story*, advancing in a gang and shaking their bicycle chains.

Later, when Spark was the only pup left, he would range further and further ahead until he could flick unnoticed over the wall and go foraging in the streets. I whistled and called but once out of sight he became hard of hearing.

Often it was Anne Stevenson who brought him back. She lived a couple of streets away and she would come out of the corner shop to find him trotting down the pavement towards her. Her own boys were teenagers then and it was as if there was some sympathy between her and the teenage Spark, some kind of understanding.

'It's difficult for him,' she would say, 'having to live in his mother's shadow. He wants to be out on his own, just mooching around, just being Sparky dog.'

Strange how secure that life seemed then. One of us always had to be there when Adam came home from school to give him his tea. The memories are of toast by the gas fire, Jaffa Cakes and chocolate fingers: so like remembering one's own childhood that it comes as something of a shock to realise that we were the parents.

Adam had spent his first nine years in a remote Cotswold valley. But he seemed to have adjusted seamlessly to this northern city and ran through the back alleys with his little marras from school. Once he spotted two of them crossing the square behind the house. He leaned out of the window and shouted in broad Sunderland, 'Hey, where yer gannin'?', then turned and asked us in his bell-like Southern English, 'Please may I go with them?'

Frances found it harder to adjust. Sometimes she would come back from shopping with the tears streaming down her cheeks. It was pure shock, an involuntary reaction to finding herself in grim, unrelenting streets, everything she had fled when she escaped the 'shabby Walthamstow' of her childhood. It was then that I remembered Kiln Hill, the farmhouse on Hadrian's Wall that Noel Connor had rented the previous year. We drove out the next weekend and rented it for the rest of the winter.

By now I have done two circuits of the park, retracing the paths I used to walk with the dogs in all weathers, sheltered under the overhang of my cap, a green, floppy cap of exaggerated proportions, the sort Rastas used to house their dreadlocks in. One fine day I appeared without it and one of the old men said, 'Where's your cap?', thought for a moment and added, 'Well, it's not really a cap, is it? More like an air-raid shelter.'

I walk out past the Art College, where freshly painted boards reflect the latest survival strategies. Something called the Reg Vardy Art Foundation has come into existence, while the Polytechnic has ditched its long-held distinction, the subject of such careful pride when I came here as Poet in Residence fourteen years ago, and become the University of Sunderland.

71

I make for the town centre, imagining that somewhere by the railway station or the bus station there might be a stall dispensing hot coffee. No such luck, I am several decades too late.

This is the New North East, where automatic doors open onto windless shopping malls. I can eat Hawaiian pancakes in a surfer's cabin or tacos in a Tijuana bar but nothing until nine o'clock. Hunched into my donkey jacket, I trudge past the plateglass windows, looking like a ghost from the bad old days when there were still pits and docks and shipyards, and workers on early shift.

Thank goodness there are still newsagents. I passed one on the way down and bought myself an ounce of Old Holborn and a packet of liquorice papers, a stand-by that goes right back to my mis-spent youth in the Sixties when

A newsagent taking in the first papers
would see us taking shape at the counter,
the ghost trade, come for Mars and Old Holborn, sugar and smoke.

I walk down to the river and cross the Span Bridge. Sit in the lee of St Peter's Church, in the relative shelter of thirteen hundred years of Christianity, and roll myself a cigarette.

The Celtic saints used to look for their place of resurrection, a solitary place on the foreshore where they could build a beehive cell and pass their days in prayer and fasting. I did not find mine until I went to Colombia seven years ago:

My fingers touch the blade

of your shoulder. And are fingers
on warm skin. We touch as only survivors

can touch.

In that new world the ground was still whole under my feet. It was as if Frances had never died, because Frances never lived there.

Now I am back, treading this ground permeated with memories. It is more like mist than earth and I wonder if England will ever feel solid again.

It used to feel all too solid. I make my way back across the Span Bridge and head for the Polytechnic, remembering how lonely that second year in Sunderland was before Frances came. I used to mark my day out in two-hour stretches, two for my own writing, two for editing, two for reviewing, and haul my way up it like a climber going from piton to piton on a rockface.

72

A course of old stone runs across one of the streets behind the Poly. The lip of a wall invites you to look over. Below is the line of an old railway, a blank white scar behind the houses. It was Bill Martin who taught me to read such signs. As we walked on Tunstall Hill, he would show me where the line used to run from Silksworth Colliery down to the South Docks, a slow-moving procession of coal trucks they would hang off as small boys, hitching a ride to school.

Bill suspected that the pithead lay under the artificial ski-slope of the new Sports Complex. When he talked, the landscaped areas around the ring road recovered their contours and I began to make sense of the names on the signposts, glimpsing the intricate pattern the pit villages had made in the days when each had its own band and marched behind its own banner at the Big Meeting.

Below this history lay the other, the monastic settlements of the seventh century that had left St Peter's there on the riverbank, in the shadow of the Boilermakers' Social Club, and its sister monastery at Jarrow under the bright blue necks of the shipyard cranes.

The monasteries came first and the towns grew up around them, a process of development preserved in Sunderland's very name: the *sundered* land, cut-off, outside the monastery wall, on the other side of the river. But to Bill there was no division: the primitive Christianity of the monasteries had surfaced again in the close community of the pit villages and their long political struggle. In his poetry he tells the story of the slogan bread, the loaves brought by miners to their comrades on strike and laid out in slogans on the hillside, and asks 'What kingdom without common feasting?' Or remembers the Big Meeting of 1951, the year of the Easington Disaster, and the 'thronged, comforting hush' when the banner, draped in black crape, was carried down onto the racecourse. Such moments become images for the sense of community we need to develop, intimations that 'Here and here is the Kingdom'.

As we drove around the North East conurbation, picking our way across the motorways to the Folk Club at Birtley on a Wednesday night, or crawling in three lanes of traffic to the Irish Centre in Newcastle on a Friday, Bill would tell me about the places we passed: Cuthbert's coffin had rested here on its way to Durham; George Stephenson built a gravity railway down that bank; Tommy Hepburn, one of the union movement's martyrs, was buried just down there.

Sometimes, in an undertone that slowly grew into a chant, like someone starting to sing under their breath and gradually gaining confidence, he would give me the outline of a new long poem. There would come a strange moment, as feature after feature of the land we were by-passing was picked out and caught up into his rapture, when the road I was following seemed to dip and climb over Bill's voice and I realised I was driving across one of the song-lines of the North.

From the Poly I have tacked round to the Durham Road. Something stops me on the corner below the garage, a memory I have to trust like an instinct, because there is no outward sign. This is the way Adam used to come home from school. There is the place where we used to stand on the kerb, clear of the corner, and look left, right and left again. I cross beside his small ghost and walk up Thornhill Park. My tired step lightens. We don't have to go the length of this road. There's an opening to the right, a shortcut.

Here it is, a narrow entry between a chainlink fence and a brick wall: the footpath beside the Comprehensive School. I follow its dogleg round and, before I know it, I am at the top of Thornhill Gardens.

The road ends in the school playing field, which means that there is no through traffic. It has a solitude, a green shade that filters down from the hundred-year-old sycamore trees into the long front gardens of the houses on the left. The air has a cool weight, like the air in a shrubbery.

Number 29, where we lived, is on the right. The front garden is a mere stub but the front door opened onto a long sweep of oak banisters, stripped oak doors and red cedar floors, white walls and dark, holly-green paint. In the months before Frances came, one of our student lodgers, John Blewitt, had completely redecorated the house, creating an interior woodland to compensate for the woods she was leaving behind in the Slad Valley.

We even turned the pantry into Frances' private bathroom. 'I can face anything,' she used to say, 'as long as I've had my bath.' It was her one indulgence, the shaping ritual of her day. For twenty minutes she would soak in hot water and mull over the night's dreams, which were the source of so much of her poetry. It was in that tiny space, lying under the miniature washbasin in a bath the width of the cupboard, that she wrote her poem for Winifred Nicholson:

> Flowers
> a dozen or more,
> I picked one summer afternoon
> from field and hedgerow.
> Resting against a wall
> I held them up
> to hide the sun.
> Cell by cell,

74

exact as dance,
I saw the colour,
structure, purpose
of each flower.
I named them with their secret names.
They flamed in air.

But, waking
I remember only two
– soapwort and figwort,
the lilac and the brown.
The rest I guess at
but cannot see
– only myself,
almost a ghost upon the road,
without accoutrement,
holding the flowers
as torch and talisman
against the coming dark.

I walk past, allowing myself just one glance. The house is up for sale.
I ring on Bill's front door and Win comes down in her dressing gown. It is eight o'clock. I have been walking for three hours.

When I sit down to take my boots off, I am surprised to see a salt-white scurf on the leather. They are crusted with sweat. I have raised blisters on each foot, thick, white quilts of swelling that I have to lance and drain.

I sit in the back garden and smoke a roll-up. Then make my way to the breakfast table, hobbling in my slippers across the thick-piled carpet.

Joan gives me her left hand, the only one she can use, and asks me to put my chair in front of her, not face-on but at an angle of about 30 degrees. Her head rests on a stiff, padded collar and looks a little to her left, which is where I need to set the chair.

Everything is ranged round her in a left-hand arc: the felt tip with which she scores out her work on the slope of the metal desk in front of her; the trolley of folders and notepads at her side.

The desk has an adjustable work surface and was made especially for her by Technical Aids. It fits around her wheelchair and looks like a modern version of the old monk's stall, a hi-tech lectern and scriptorium.

When I sit down, only Joan's head and shoulders are visible above its struts and bars. It's intimidating to look up from my easy chair and see her sat there in involuntary state. Almost like meeting the Queen out of *Alice*. Or a talking head out of a Beckett play, the writer imprisoned in her own constructions.

I'm glad we talked first on the phone and that I came here with a sense of her personality already vivid in my head.

One of the first poems Joan shows me reflects on the way a wheelchair forms a 'touch barrier':

> too high for a child to reach,
> too low for man to bend,
>> to condescend
>> to comprehend

More bitter still, for Joan herself, is her inability to reach out and touch those she loves. There are times when she can see John worn down by the effort of looking after her, as he has for the last sixteen years. She longs to be able to rise from the wheelchair, walk across the room and give him a hug. Instead she can only whisper, 'Sorry.' Cold flat 'Sorry.'

I am reminded of a dream Frances had during her last few weeks in hospital. She was waltzing with Laurence Olivier, pressed close to him and waltzing. In other dreams a man had summoned her, a distinguished black diplomat, a man of great presence and power. She felt very drawn to him but she had to say, 'No, I cannot come with you, I must stay with my husband and child.' We had wondered if the black man was Death. So now we wondered if Laurence Olivier wasn't Death in another guise, if she wasn't dancing with Death. Then Frances cut through all the talk of symbols and archetypes. 'What it really was,' she said, 'was simply the longing to be touched, to be held. It's so lonely lying here in this hospital bed, I just long for someone to come and take me in their arms.'

I tell Joan this story and she shows me a poem where she is introduced to Katie, the young daughter of one of her carers, who stares at her with large grave eyes:

> I'm sitting high,
> she's standing low.
> I'm wheelchaired, highcollared,
>> Katie's just three
>>>> (wish she could see the normal old me)
> pressed to her brother seeking protection
>> eyes locked in my direction.

I'm unaware
like tortoise she creeps,
appears at my side whilst I wonder why,
lifts gentle my hand like some charming count,
light-kisses the back with such grave attention
 I smile in affection

In another poem Joan is watching Katie turn somersaults on the lawn. 'Wish I could do that,' she says wistfully. And back comes the child's reply, so sensitive and so matter-of-fact that it reaches, like that kiss on the back of the hand, across all the barriers of age and infirmity:

You could if you were five like me
and didn't have to sit in that wheelchair.

The council have found me a flat, a one-bedroomed upstairs flat, quiet and comfortable. It's in Seghill, a name I recognise from railway history. A waggon-way was opened from Seghill to Backworth when the Cramlington Coal Company could not get enough coal to the Tyne on the existing track. The pit is closed now but you still drive over the railway line when you come in from Blyth.

I fetch a mattress and some kitchen things from Ladywell, buy some furniture from a secondhand shop in Blyth, and find some ornaments on the tideline at Seaton Sluice and Druridge Bay: two skate's eggs with long curling horns that make them look like beetles from outer space; a piece of old china plate that's been worn into a willow pattern pebble; an owl-eyed stone; the stump of a green glass bottle that says *Water, Forbes Street, Aberdeen*; part of a stone jar that says *SEHOLD AMMONIA*; fragments of salt-frosted glass, white, green and purple, and a piece of coal that's been smoothed and rounded into a bright mineral beauty.

The days begin to fall into a pattern. Each morning I walk past the paper shop, turn down an asphalt track that's strewn with an abandoned jacket and several pairs of old boots, pass a scrapyard with chickens and head out onto a footpath between fields. For twenty minutes I walk back into the world's first morning, my eye quickening with the wind's movement through corn and the shards of blue sky in the puddles. Once the old hunter-gatherer in me is awake, I force myself to turn for home and find a path across the whiteness of the page.

I am working on my first prose book, an account of the misadventures by which I stumbled into poetry. I have just reached the summer of 1966, when I fell in love for the first time:

She was standing in front of me, no more than child-high, the round head between the straight curtains of hair tilted as she looked up at the map. I saw the curve of the cheekbone, the fineness of the cheek moulding round to the chin, and felt the horizon contract to a small vertical, perhaps five-foot-two.

I remember the quietness of the streets at that moment. The traffic of the day had died down and it would be another hour before the pavements filled with couples out for the evening, knots of students on their way to the *Scala*, bevies of drinkers crowding into pub passageways. The day was in suspense – and the suspense held for a moment as the surprise filtered through. She was bone perfect, just enough of an oval in the line of the jaw to balance the round head and the broad cheekbones.

That was important to me then. Later it ceased to matter, and I lived in the changing expressions of her face, in her different ages: the clouded forehead of a serious child, the woman's humour that stirred in the long line of the lips. Most of all, perhaps, in her eyes' river-light and shadow. But what I saw at first glance was a sculpted Saxon head, a bone helmet I could set beside Modigliani's Jeanne or Picasso's Sylvette, posters that hung on student walls all over Oxford.

I looked into myself and thought: Don't lose her. It was as if I was back in Beech Wood before dawn. Everything in me concentrated and became still.

Later that summer I hitch-hiked to the South of France where she had told me she would be staying on a beach with her friend Hannah:

I could only see into the middle distance. Beyond that the sand shimmered and went out of focus. Spots slid across my eyes. No doubt they were sunbathers too.

It was like trying to find two dots in the Milky Way.

I stepped out onto the sand and a wolf-whistle went up. A thousand pairs of sunglasses swivelled in my direction. *Wretched Boater*, I thought. But it wasn't the boater. On the beach, in the midday sun, that looked almost sensible. It was the hair, the blond pelt curling to my shoulders. The angel's mane, as Anke once called it, in one of her inspired bendings of English. They had never seen anything like it. Or only in photos of the one French rock singer to cash in on the beatnik vogue. His name began to rise all around me, in long, derisive jets of sound: *Antoine! Antoine!*.

Children pointed and shrieked, dancing on the edge of their family circles. Deckchairs leaned back to consider me over their *apéritifs.* Sunglasses dandled their smiles, curious, amused, mocking. Oiled backs sat up like seals, stretching their necks to look at me. I dodged between them, scanning the horizon for that one proud head with its straight fall of hair.

In the end a Catalan took me under his wing, a much-travelled man who had a stall selling antiques in the marketplace:

'Have you seen them?' I asked. 'Two Dutch girls, one with long blonde hair, the other with ginger ringlets. I've been looking for them for two days now.' Desperation must have shrilled in my voice because he said, 'Ne t'en fais pas!' and began to tell me a story. He had been in the French Foreign Legion, marching in a column of men through a little town in North Africa, when he saw a girl gazing at him from the pavement. Their eyes met and she threw him a rose. As they marched away, a song came into his head.

By now he was gripping my elbow, his eyes burning into me:

'The girl sees the man, just for an instant. She throws him the rose. But he is a soldier, he can't break step, he has to march away. In that instant, something in her dies.'

He sang me the song as the crowd broke around us. It began gently, sadly, as though it would become a lament, then broke into a note so high it sounded transparent, a note washed clear of longing or loss.

I am just writing this when a letter comes from Colombia. I returned to England at the end of January. It is now July. Before I can go to Colombia again, it will be the end of December. The separations are getting longer as we run out of money. I have been trying to resolve the situation. I have been thinking of selling Ladywell so that I can settle in Colombia.

Gently but firmly the letter tells me not to. Then we would both lose our independence. Let's resolve it another way, the letter says. Let's just be friends.

Out come the tobacco and the liquorice papers. Back come the sleepless nights. Dawn finds me walking the beach at Seaton Sluice, watching the fishermen brace their rods against the morning tide and wondering if I have learned anything in the twenty seven years since I walked the beach at Barcarès. Perhaps only where to look for the songs that you need at such times. I put on my tape of Atahualpa Yupanqui, the Argentinian folk-singer. There is one song where he rides away through the snow at the end of a relationship. As he rides, he sings quietly to himself and his voice has dignity, self-possession:

Estos frios nunca matan.
Tampoco mata el dolor.
Rigores ya no me asustan.
Se andar solo y sin amor.

I start to translate the song, as if, by finding the words for its strengths, I can make them mine:

> Cold such as this never kills
> and neither will sorrow.
> I have learned to keep my nerve
> in the wastes below zero.
> I know how to travel
> alone without love.

'Writing about visit to Turkey', says the memo, and gives a woman's name and number. I am already bristling as I tap out the digits on the office phone, imagining some pushy woman with ambitions to be a travel writer, who wants me to help her knock an article into shape.

The voice that answers is hesitant, confiding. I can hear the notes forming on the breath, the recorder music of old age. To me she does not say 'Turkey', she talks of 'the Dardanelles'. She explains that her father was lost there in the First World War and I realise that she means at Gallipoli.

She is eighty now. The first thing she remembers as a child is her mother going into hysterics when she received the telegram. Her father was 'missing believed killed'. The body was never found and for years her mother used to worry that he might still be out there somewhere, wandering around in a state of shock. It was the uncertainty that haunted her, the not knowing what had happened to him. As David Constantine puts it in the sequence of poems he wrote for his grandmother, whose husband went missing in the trenches:

> There being no grave, there being not even one
> Ranked among millions somewhere in France,
> Her grief went without where to lay its head.

It was a grief the daughter inherited as she grew up. She wrote to the War Office for more information, in the hope of putting her mother's mind at rest. All they could tell her was the number of the plaque in the military cemetery where her father's name was recorded. She wanted to take her mother to see it but the fare was beyond them. Not until her mother was dead, and she herself was in her sixties, was she able to make the journey. She felt she was making it for the whole family and she's written an account of it in case it can be of help to other families who have suffered a similar loss.

She calls at the Forum next day, a pretty, grey-haired lady in a dark blue three-quarter length jacket, so beautifully cut that I compliment her on it. She tells me she made it herself, from some material she bought at a sale of work, and shows me the silver badge she wears on the lapel. It has an anchor, the inscription *Collingwood* in gold letters, and three entwined capitals, *RND*: the initials of her father's unit, the Royal Naval Division.

All sorts of details move me as I read through the hand-written sheets of lined, blue notepaper. Mrs Cessford's own courage in setting off for Istanbul: she had never been abroad before and her sister was sure she would be killed. The Turks' many kindnesses to her, springing from a culture where the old are still respected, and the generous inscription in the Dardanelles Museum, explaining that the Turkish people value enemy soldiers buried there as if they were their own sons. The visit was a healing experience and she went back twice. But what moves me most is the lifelong remembrance, the ancient ritual of mourning finally completed by means of the travel agency and the chartered flight. It is a glimpse into the wounded body of humanity, patiently working to repair the tissues torn by war. Sixty years after the Lords of the Admiralty dispatch their fleet, the men's families are still laying them to rest, and an old lady sets out from Ashington to make her pilgrimage to the Dardanelles.

Marjorie waits in her wheelchair in the cathedral cloisters while I go down the steps to the refectory and bring our tea and scones up on a tray. There must be a disabled access down there somewhere because I can see a disabled toilet but there are no signs to it from the cloisters. Wheeling Marjorie round the cathedral has been rather like playing snakes and ladders: there are ramps but they take us in maddeningly short circles and we keep landing back where we started from. We are able to make our pilgrimage to the Tomb of the Venerable Bede but not to the Shrine of St Cuthbert, whose cathedral this is.

But it was worth the journey simply to hear Marjorie's intake of breath as we came out of the sunlight of the Cathedral Close into the great dimmed vault of the nave. Few places on earth are as numinous as this. I say 'on earth' but the sensation is of being under the earth, in one of those womb-shaped barrows where our ancestors laid their dead to await rebirth. Were the Celtic saints undertaking the same journey in their places of resurrection? Is there a link between the barrow and the beehive cell?

In the years of our friendship, long before we became lovers, I took Frances to Penmon Priory, on the north-eastern tip of Anglesey, another Celtic monastery taken over by the Normans. At Penmon there is the sense of a complete break, an antagonism, almost, between the stone barracks of the Augustinian friars and the solitary cells of the Celtic monks down at the sea's edge. At Durham there is no sense of a break. A Celtic line of endless renewal, the line we call interlace, runs from barrow to cell and on into the rounded arch of the Romanesque. The rounded arch is humbler than the pointed arch. It does not point us to the sky. It bows its head and returns us to the earth.

> well of silence
> beehive cell
> at the sea's edge

– lines I once wrote about Penmon. They merge in my mind with a luminous fact culled from a reading at the Morden Tower: the central chamber that gives a buoy its stability, the cavity where opposing waves wash in and cancel each other out, is called a stilling well.

For me writing begins as a recovery of silence. It begins as listening. When I drove out to Kiln Hill, the farmhouse on Hadrian's Wall, the first thing I would do was light a fire in the small sitting room where I wrote. It was so quiet that I could hear the tinkling of the coals as they caught and that quickly-vanished rhythm would attune my ear, a breath that rose and went.

Frances liked to sit up late over a dying fire until the waking mind was lulled into a half-sleep, a kind of trance out of which words would come. By day she would go for long walks, taking the steep track down from Birdoswald to the Irthing Valley. She liked to watch the river move across its floodplain,

> glimmer of oils
> over roots and sodden grass,

forming small whirlpools on the underside of rocks that were 'wind become visible'. On stormy nights in Kiln Hill we had the reverse impression: the house was a sharp rock standing up in mid-stream and we listened as wave after wave broke on the gable end and licked under the eaves.

We could only afford the house in winter, when the wind along the Wall was a shock in the ear. To drop down into the Valley was to drop down out of the wind, which may explain its curiously intent atmosphere, what Frances called 'a charged stillness'. There is another explanation. At this point the Irthing, which has been flowing through sandstone, comes up against limestone. It twists around the sill and ricochets off the other side, throwing up two crescents of silt, two curves of flat, fertile land under a limestone cliff, which the Celts called Camboglanna, the Crooked Glen. The name has led some to believe that it may have been the site of Arthur's last battle, the Battle of Camlann. Frances took the hint and gave the details she had noted on her walks another resonance, combining them with Bedivere's replies to the dying Arthur when he sends him to throw Excalibur back into the Lake. Bedivere cannot bear to part with the sword. Twice he goes down to the water's edge and twice he returns without throwing it in – a deception that comes to light as soon as Arthur asks him what he saw.

> *I saw nothing but waves and winds*

> . . . the moon resting in a broken apple tree
> an ushering wind shake ash and alder
>   by the puckered river.
> Lightly, like boats, the thin leaves rock and spin.

> Blood-dark berries stir; above my head the thorn trees lean.
> In their black pools the moon fragments itself.

> Ghost dry the unquiet reeds . . .

> *I saw nothing but the waters wap*
> *and waves wan*

In the end, though, what drew Frances to the Valley was not myth or history, not any human quality: it was the bareness of the place, its integrity,

> a field of stones
> a river of stones

> each stone in its place

Cattle were grazed there. Rabbits burrowed and foxes hunted. Deer came down to the water to drink. Otherwise it was left to itself, a natural oratory where walking was a form of prayer and Frances could rise from her bones as surely as any Celtic saint in his place of resurrection:

between air and water

my shadow

laving the stones

The dene. A word I had not met until I came to the North East. It comes from the Old English *denu*, a vale or broad valley, and was once widespread, not only in place-names such as Taunton Dene, but in metaphorical expressions: death's dene, or the dene of tears.

Now it has shrunk in size and range. It has come to mean 'the deep, narrow and wooded vale of a rivulet' and has no place in everyday speech outside Durham and Northumberland. Here it is an evocative word, a word cherished in people's memories. When the North East was covered in pit-heads and pit-heaps, the little, wooded valleys that run down to the coast were all that was left of the wild, the only places where kids could play and young couples court and old people walk on a Sunday afternoon. 'The dene' means to a Northeasterner what 'the green' or 'the common' or 'the rec' means to a Southerner.

Sunday afternoon and a steady stream of cars is turning off the Seghill Road and driving up to the council tip with bootloads of garden rubbish and DIY debris – a new tradition in which I, as a council tenant with no garden, take no part. A newly-erected gate and a freshly-laid gravel path, the creation of an enlightened councillor, take me down into the dene, where the path dips between brambles and climbs under stunted oaks. No need to mark it now. Every blackberry bush has a skirt of trodden earth, every tree root a rubbed shine. By the time I come out into the fields behind Seaton Delaval, I am walking in company, aware of everyone who walked here before me, the miners of Seghill and Holywell who played here as lads and courted their lasses here and walked here with their families, watch-chains shining on the waistcoats of their Sunday suits.

Late September. Already the light is withdrawing. It lingers on the gnarled bark of a tree's shoulder while the burn is in shadow, soundless and chill in its black bed. At this time I used to fly to Colombia. Perpetual spring in the mountains. Perpetual summer in the valleys below. Now I am on the edge of these flat fields as they shelve into autumn.

Someone is crossing in front of me. A woman with a pail of blackberries. I join her on the network of paths, remembering that, if I strike left, I can reach the café in Seaton Delaval before closing time. I can join the thinning queue under the Craven A clock and order a Double Nougat, a block of vanilla ice-cream pressed between two half-inch thick wafers of chocolate nougat. You lick as it drips and get chocolate all over your cheeks and chin.

From the Ridge

1 HOOFPRINTS

after a song by Atahualpa Yupanqui

Snow at the head of the valley.
A woman chooses her time.
And do I trudge sadly away?
No, I saddle up a line
from an old ballad, I go
With a good horse under me . . .

      Hoofprints, hoofprints, little hoofprints
      of my pride. All that's left of me.
      I gave her all I am.

Cold such as this never kills
and neither will sorrow.
Don't lose your nerve
in the wastes below zero.
Learn how to travel
alone without love.

      Hoofprints, hoofprints, little hoofprints
      of my heart. Cupped flames I follow,
      lit hollows in the snow.

2 THE JOURNEY

I had to go on
without me,

let the horse
pick its way

on the glitters
of gradient,

the nameless paths
of the ice melt.

85

I was the ghost
of a devotion,

head bowed
without a prayer.

The chalk
of a small town

frayed into rock.
A dog barked,

tireless as the creak
of a wheel.

We forded the sun
on the ridge,

my sad bones
sunk in their sack

as the long bones
stepped delicately

out of their own
shadow.

3 SPLINTERS
  after a song by Atahualpa Yupanqui

They are company
of a kind,
these splinters I am feeding
to the fire:

something said under her breath,
something breathed in her sleep.

They are constancy
of a kind,
these hill paths I have chosen
at every turn:

somewhere our spirits walk,
somewhere we talk in our sleep.

4 SKETCHES

I cannot tear myself
from the skim of sunlight
on the wall, slow-

dawning and provisional
as her shuffle to the stove
in a dressing-gown, her face

still smudged with sleep. Only
watch out of the first warmth
as she heats water in a pan

and strains it through coffee
in a cotton sock. Only wait
for the head to lift from the cup,

for the eyes to look out of
their aftermath, disbelieving
and resolute. A line wakes

in her then. It squares
the shoulders against gravity
and curves into the small

of the back: just the stance
she has at the mirror,
stretching up to the wand

of mascara, her spine
hollowed into
the branching crease

of a birch; just the stance
she has at the easel,
waist wrapped in a towel

and shoulders working
like a boxer drubbing
at the overhead ball;

and just the stance she lost
as we edged along the stalls
in the market, her hair up

under a flat cap, her head
bent to the anxieties
of thrift; small, tensed body

I would shelter from the wind
with my body, and can only
watch for now, watch

from first light on the wall.

5 THE DESCENT

I am glad of the slip
and slide of a hoof,
of another breath
beside me, as we go
dismounted, shoulder
to shoulder down
the rock. Nothing
but the airless cliff
and cloud shadows still
as coal seams. Nothing
but the compressions
of the strata. Only
my own company,
the voices I can hear
under my breath: hers
dark, with such *brio*
every word has its
animal life; one honed
to an edge of light;
and some with sadness
in their very timbre,

Chavela Vargas
singing to her black dove,
the unholy ghost
of all her benders,
Bola de Nieve
holding to a love
against the forces of
la ley y la razón;
all interwoven
and all worn into
the song of the path,
one breath of many.

Notes

Atahualpa Yupanqui was an Argentinian folksinger who took a Native American name as a way of championing Native American rights. His songs create their own austere landcape, though he died in exile in Paris.

Chavela Vargas is a Mexican folksinger who has written some of the most erotic songs one woman has ever addressed to another. *Paloma Negra*, her most famous song, manages to be humorous and heartbreaking, tender in one breath and fierce in the next.

Bola de Nieve (Snowball) was a Cuban cabaret singer and pianist, admired by Hemingway and by many writers and artists of that generation. Like Billy Strayhorn, he had to live out a double minority, being black and gay.

I came to know the Yupanqui songs as songs, listening to them on a creaky old tape, and I have never seen a printed text. I worked from the images they left in my mind and anyone who knows the original songs will see that I have completely remade them, but in homage to Atahualpa Yupanqui, apprenticing myself to his spirit.
    One phrase, I have to confess, I misunderstood. I took *huella* to mean hoofprint, which seemed natural enough in a song about a man riding away on horseback. But when I came to perform my version with two Colombian guitarists, they told me of another sense of *huella*, which is not in the dictionary, and possibly unknown outside Argentina, except to musicians. The *huella* is the path across the pampas – a track worn long before Columbus came – and a song-form in Argentinian music, the song you make as you ride along the path. The song I had translated is itself a *huella*.
    This was such a profound and lovely meaning that I was left in a real quandary. I wanted to incorporate it – who wouldn't? – but that would mean losing
            Hoofprints, hoofprints, little hoofprints
                of my pride
which was, I suspected, the very line that made my version work. I did start to dismantle it and try out new choruses,
            Ancient path, beaten path, path
                Of my song
until the poet Jackie Litherland, who had been at that performance, told me to leave well alone. There is such a thing, she pointed out, as a lucky mistake.
    The image of the *huella* stayed with me, though, and proved to be just what I needed to manage 'The Descent'.

89

FURTHER EXTRACTS FROM THE JOURNAL OF A RESIDENCY

Sleepless nights send me surfing through the days, tilting this way and that to keep myself upright. Sometimes I need a cigarette, sometimes a cup of strong black tea.

Strange weather is coming in off the sea, a still, colourless cold, heavy with salt, like a sea fret without fog.

By the end of the morning the cold is inside me and I feel my energy start to gutter. Not so much tiredness as panic, a flickering of identity, like a candle that's about to be blown out. What I need is a shot of whisky.

I remember the Flying Horse, the pub up the road where I have been told the local musicians meet.

'Can get a bit hairy on a Saturday night,' my informant said, 'but it's okay.'

The first entry to a pub is always difficult, particularly in a small town: every eye tends to turn and fix on the stranger.

The Flying Horse is almost empty. Just five or six young people gathered at the near end of the bar. I walk past them and begin to scan the optics.

A girl with a short helmet of hair, almost an urchin cut, and large, clear, intelligent eyes detaches herself from the group and comes to take my order.

Mackinlays? No. Three Barrels? No. Then I spot some familiar print upside-down.

'What's that bottle, the one on the end?'

'Rebel Yell.'

'That's a bourbon, isn't it?'

She nods. 'A double for one sixty.'

'Brilliant. With one cube of ice, please.'

Rebel Yell doesn't need more. It's a pretty waterish bourbon. I take my donkey jacket off and throw it onto the nearest bench. Slump wearily on the bench myself and begin to roll a cigarette.

Then I become aware of the difference. These kids aren't staring at me. They've smiled and turned back to their conversation.

This pub is alright. I can come here again.

I drop into the Flying Horse for a drink after work. A small man in a grubby white T-shirt and an old black leather jacket is sitting on the customers' side of the bar. From the tousled black hair and the two days' growth of black stubble I assume that he must be the landlord. No one would go out looking like that.

He leans on his elbows, crouched over the ashtray in front of him, and sips from a large, heavily diluted whisky.

There's a different barmaid, a blonde girl called Alison whom I recognise from the Forum: she's an artist and she's painting a mural for one of the community centres. She stands there with a full bottle of whisky in her hands and looks up at the empty on the optic.

'Stevie,' she says, 'I can't remember how to do this.'

Teeth shine out of the dark stubble as he throws his head back. Eyes gleam under the half-closed lids.

'You have the IQ of a toothbrush,' he informs her, 'and the mental agility of a small soapdish.'

A Scots accent gives the words a peculiar precision. They take shape on the air, each one edged with a tender malice.

Alison beams at him. Obviously she's heard it all before. He descends from his stool with a great show of weariness and stamps round the bar to change the optic.

'Women ought to be chopped into one-inch cubes and fed to the dogs. Then at least they'd be good for something.'

The next day I drop into the Flying Horse at lunchtime. I fancy a ginger beer to drink with my stotties. Steve is quite put out.

'I order the ginger beer for myself,' he says.

The pub is almost deserted and Steve is over the customers' side of the bar, minding his young son Fergus, who is still strapped into his baby buggy. The bottom of the buggy is piled, not with shopping but with books. I squat down to read the titles, expecting to find Jack Higgins and Alistair Maclean. Instead I see Spinoza. Aristotle's *Nicomachean Ethics*. The plays of Sheridan. The collected stories of Sir Arthur Conan Doyle.

The only lapse is a copy of *The Silmarillion*. I remark on this to Steve and he shrugs his shoulders:

'They were just some books I picked up in a sale. But you can say this for Tolkien, he almost has what Conan Doyle has, the power to create a narrative that has universal appeal, that becomes a kind of myth. You can say Sherlock Holmes to anyone, anywhere in the world and they'll know who you mean. They'll see a man with a bent pipe and they'll imagine a hansom cab moving through the fog – even if they've never seen fog and they've no idea what a hansom cab is.'

I have only to think of my time in Colombia to realise that he is right. There is always mist at the edge of Bogotá's high plateau, where warm air from the valleys below condenses and hangs in clouds among the pine trees. Whenever we drove through its chill, white silence, someone would say, 'Just like the stories of Sherlock Holmes.'

'The irony is,' Steve continues, 'that Conan Doyle could never do it again. He wrote all sorts of other stories, but none of them have that quality. The Sherlock Holmes stories are quite short. He only has a page or two to set things up. But you can read any of them and for the first seven hundred words there's not a word out of place. It's a kind of poetry.'

Saturday afternoon and the pub is filling up. Steve is behind the bar, moving quickly from customer to customer. He leans towards me to catch my order, swings away to put a glass up to the optic and swings back, taking my money with the other hand. He breaks from the till like a scrum-half from the scrum, head ducked and already turning to the next customer.

Later there's a lull. Everyone is settled around the bar, leaning on their elbows and talking over their drinks, and Steve treads the space in front of the optics like someone treading water, leaning back and pushing his feet against the floor in a slow, swaying halfstep, a dance of unwinding. After so many quick glances up and out across the bar, he looks down into himself and smiles. The voices surge around him and the tape pounds overhead. He sketches a beat with his hands. He could be dancing to the tape but really he is dancing to the music he likes best, the rhythms of the pub, 'the music of what happens'.

'How are you, Steve?' I shout across the bar.

'Oh,' he says, 'tenaciously frolicking.'

Saturday again. An unfamiliar feeling of freedom. For twenty years I have been a freelance writer, more or less ignoring weekends and bank holidays. If anything, I saw them as providing ideal working conditions, days when I could hole up in my cottage and write, secure in the knowledge that the phone would not ring.

Now, after five days of compressing my writing into the mornings and my appointments into the afternoons, up pops Saturday, a little, unaccountable festival, whose hours are not logged in my office diary: high day and holiday of the unknown god.

The question is, what shall I do with it? I seem to have lost the knack of solitude. It keeps shelving into loneliness. Perhaps I'd be better off in the Flying Horse, sipping a ginger beer with my stotties and letting the life of the pub flow around me.

By now I'm known there. Steve has a couple of books behind the bar, a copy of my last book of poems, *Given Ground*, and a copy of Frances' *Collected Poems*. Sometimes in the early evening, when the pub is quiet, I come in to find the barmaid sitting up on her high stool, a drink in front of her, a cigarette in her hand, and one of the books open on her lap.

Mostly, I have to say, it's Frances' book.

'It's just natural curiosity,' Rosemary explains to me, 'You think, "Oh, another woman", and you want to know what she's experienced, what she's felt.'

Rosemary's a photographer and works one or two nights behind the bar. None of the barmaids works more than twelve hours a week and I am still putting names to the changing faces: the one with the haze of brown ringlets, like an Edwardian beauty who's just let her hair down, is Lil; the one who served me on my first day, the girl with the short helmet of hair and the large, clear, intelligent eyes, is Sandra. Only now she's dispensed with the helmet, almost dispensed with hair altogether, and looks at me from under the flat top of a crew-cut, a neat triangle of bristles tipped with silver. The effect is oddly becoming.

'Sandra,' I warn her, 'you're going to play havoc with my gender associations. I shall find myself smiling at GI's.'

Today there is a new silhouette behind the bar, a slim woman with short, dark, curly hair. As she turns, there is a glimmer of white and silver: full moon of her face, zodiac of her earrings, white pool of her neck in a low-cut T-shirt. The light-blue jeans are casual and the dove-grey T-shirt discreet, cut in a crew-neck rather than a V-neck, but she seems stage-lit. It must be the earrings, great planetry wheels of silver with cloud shimmers of pendants, that have turned the bar into a cabaret.

'Steve,' I ask, 'who is this lovely lady?'

He pauses, framing his answer, and the woman smiles:

'Steve doesn't see any lovely lady.'

'This,' he pronounces finally, 'is Agnes. Miss Agnes Peabody.'

'Oh, come on now, Steve!' I protest, 'there are many ways of describing her body but Peabody isn't one of them.'

Later, when he goes off to join the card school, we're left alone at the bar.

'What do they really call you?' I ask her.

'Susan.'

I discover that she's from Blyth but lives in Sunderland with her boyfriend. He brings her over on the back of his motorbike. Like most of the women who work behind the bar, she's bringing up a child and

I begin to see the reason for the low-cut T-shirt and the starry earrings. After a week's attendance on a small boy's unruly energies, a week of scrubbing his knees, squeezing his spots and washing his clothes, it must restore her to have a Saturday afternoon's glamour, to powder her face, arrange her hair in a dark halo behind the earrings, and step out into the small O of the bar.

She's working the right shift. Everyone in the Horse looks theatrical on a Saturday. Lads in vests and baseball caps sweep in off the streets of New York, thin braids woven into the long hair falling to their shoulders. There's a pirate edition of Andy Warhol, his hair tinted and cut high on the head, leaving just a silvery blond quiff. But when a Horse Lord strides in, dreadlocks drawn tight to the back of his head so that they spring out behind him like a stallion's tail, I know we have passed beyond MTV into some realm of free association where Tolkien meets Mad Max.

They sit in a big circle around the tables in front of the bar. A shine comes off them, an energy they have yet to learn how to use. Only half-aware of it, only aware it intensifies when they are together, they look across at each other with a kind of shared elation, a generation coming into its own.

It must be out of courtesy towards me that the conversation turns to poetry. And turns more naturally than it might in literary circles. No gossip here. No defensiveness. No hissing of names or dismantling of reputations. Almost at once we are talking in earnest. It is as if, simply by being a poet, I confirm something in them, an instinct they usually have to keep hidden, or even suppress.

Colin, another photographer, quotes a line of Wordsworth he remembers from school, about gathering hazelnuts:

> Touch – for there is a spirit in the woods.

Janet, who works for Eagle Star, confesses that she did not hand her set books in after English A Level because she could not bear to be parted from them. The school Wordsworth still sits up on her shelf, a wicket gate into the lost land of the imagination.

The big circle in the Horse Saturday lunchtime seems to radiate from the corner where Rosemary sits, shopping bags all around her, hand-bag open on her lap, talking and lighting a cigarette. On the table in front of her is a pint of Snakebite.

Half an hour's calm amid the flurry. Half an hour's ease, to which she gives herself so completely that she seems to embody it.

What's that song Paul Young sings?

> *Wherever I lay my hat,*
> *that's my home.*

Some women have the opposite gift. They make a home wherever they sit.

'You're looking better!'

'You should have seen me ten minutes ago, trying to lug my shopping up the street. I was almost bent double out there on the pavement. I thought my back was going to lock. Thank goodness Steve came along. He brought me in and sat me down. He says I'm not to walk another step. He's going to ring for a taxi.

I tell her to forget the taxi. The car's outside the Forum. I'll run her home when she's ready.

I hover over the corner till the Horselord moves up and makes room for me on the bench. Rosemary whispers in my ear and he gives us a curious glance. How come we're such good friends all of a sudden?

What she's telling me is that the lad on the other side of him is Yeti, the young painter I've been waiting to meet.

I noticed him once before and thought of Isherwood's *I Am a Camera*. Only now it would be a movie camera or a video camera, one left running by Andy Warhol. Everything in him flows back to the head, which is screened by the peak of a US Army cap, worn low over the forehead, and the dark, oblong slits of his sunglasses. He floats into the Horse on a long stride, hands in his pockets, and would seem laid back if you were not aware of the video head recording you as part of the world's passing show.

When the Horselord takes their glasses up to the bar, I move along the bench and introduce myself. I explain that I've worked with painters in the past and would like to see something of his.,

'I don't have much around at the moment. Most of my stuff's in my portfolio up at the College. But I'm working on something for Steve. You're welcome to look at the drawings for that.'

There are two Flying Horses in the pub already, both done by customers: a Pegasus soaring against streaks of crayon and a dramatic picture of a horse rearing and spreading its wings, about to take off. Steve has commissioned a third from Yeti and the rumour is that he's come up with something quite different.

We wait until there is a lull and move off, carrying Rosemary's shopping between us. She's intrigued: she's never been to Yeti's studio before.

It's in a sidestreet off the Waterloo Road, a small block of flats as bleak as a tower block: graffiti run up the concrete stairs. Once through the metal door, the surfaces soften: the sofa's draped in velvet and there are cushions scattered everywhere. It could be a hippy pad in the Sixties. One room is dominated by a twentieth-century totem, built by Yeti's brother out of bits of junk. You look for a face and meet the wide blank eyes of a gas mask, a godlike stare and a piglike snout.

Another room is dominated by the easel on which Yeti is painting his Flying Horse. It *is* different. The horse is upright, a man with a horse's head, hooves and a tail. Not a Centaur in reverse, for Centaurs are usually shown as old and wise, but a Minohippos, an equine version of the Minotaur, powerful and troubled. A dragonfly's spine arches over him, a mythic jetpack by which he is steering himself down onto a stage. He could be a rock star making a dramatic entrance at an open air concert, descending out of green shadows into a red spotlight.

It is the lighting that is giving Yeti problems. The torso, which should be ridges of hard muscle where the horse hangs from the dragonfly, is a blur where the oils have been worked and reworked. But there is one drawing where the image has come clear and the Horse-god, as Yeti calls him, makes a perfect slow landing, slightly crouched against the upward pull of his flying machine. One leg is thrust into the foreground, a tense line running down through the fetlock to the hoof.

Yeti points out a weakness, a problem of perspective in the thigh he has yet to resolve, but it is still a striking drawing. I offer him £10 for it and he signs it with his real name, Darren Yates.

The afternoon has ended well for us both. What I like about painters is that they don't hunch over their ideas, hiding them away in notebooks as poets do. They pin them up on the wall and look at them: 'What's all this about, then?' It's that amused detachment that attracts me, the way they accept the imagination as a natural phenomenon and let it blow across their walls like wind and weather.

Though Yeti seems a little alarmed by the storm in his head. 'I can't imagine what I'll be like when I'm forty,' he says to me, as if he's afraid it'll have blown him away by then. Or blown out altogether and left him as someone else, someone he can't recognise.

'You'll be just the same as you are now,' I tell him, 'only a little calmer. Better able to carry out your ideas.'

Cut to the beach at dawn after a sleepless night.

Early evening in the Flying Horse. My favourite time, when the pub is quiet. I like to drop in after work and stand at the bar for an hour, chatting and savouring a malt whisky. Then home to the flat, where I put a blues tape on the cheap machine I bought for my sojourn here and cook myself a meal. Fish is so fresh and cheap that I eat it all the

time: mackerel, herrings, Craster kippers, or gurnards, a strange, prim-
itive-looking fish with jaws like a piranha that I have discovered here
in Blyth. I buy them in pairs, headed and skinned: two torpedoes of
rich, firm flesh that I wrap in foil with garlic and butter and bake for a
few minutes in a hot oven.

Steve can never understand why I vary my whiskies, drinking
Talisker one evening and Inchgower the next.

'What is the point,' I ask, 'of having so many malts if you don't ring
the changes?'

I point to his own curious drinking habits, rum and coke one night,
whisky and lemonade the next.

'The truth is,' he confesses, 'that I don't like any of them. Deep
down, I loathe alcohol. I detest it. There's not a single drink I could
say I really liked. Not one. They're a penance, that's what they are. Just
different forms of penance. You do it daily and once a month, if you're
lucky, you get a moment's illumination.'

Time to put Fergus to bed. He goes upstairs and leaves Sandra in
charge.

Just three of us in her corner and a big man drinking alone at the
other end of the bar.

Sandra and Michelle are in their early twenties and both going
through a divorce. They put their heads together while I chat to
Emma, who's eighteen and works in a factory. There's something
about her I like, a kind of stubborn self-possession.

A punk virtue, expressed in her hair, which is shaved even closer
than Sandra's and ends in a tiny wedge of bristles, so pale they are
almost transparent. She is wondering what to tint them. Not silver.
Everyone does that. I suggest palomino: dark brown tipped with
white. She gives it some thought. She likes that idea.

We stand in a companionable silence, sipping our drinks and
listening to the music on the tape deck, a succession of golden oldies
selected by Sandra. The rhythms build until we are swaying to them,
dancing on the spot. Sandra and Michelle look up from their confab,
the big man raises his glass and smiles, and music flows the length of
the bar until time is almost visible, an element in which we are moving
as easily as buzzards turning on a thermal or fish fanning out across a
sunlit shallows.

By the time I have cleared my office and packed everything into the
car, it is late on Saturday afternoon. I lock the building and push the
keys back through the letterbox. Only one thing remains. To say good-
bye to the Flying Horse.

It must be later than I thought. Susan has come off-duty and is round the customers' side of the bar, wild-eyed and white in the face. The cabaret sheen has gone and she is a tired woman at the end of her shift, having two or three quick drinks before she rides home on the pillion. She catches sight of me and rushes up to a man in a motorbike jacket who is standing waiting, helmet under his arm.

'Ray,' she says, 'I want you to meet Roger. He's a poet and he was married to another poet and she died and they hadn't been together long and, anyway, it was all just tragic. There's one of her poems that's really beautiful. What was it now? I liked it so much that I wrote it down.'

She fetches her handbag from behind the bar and begins to hunt through it. Flips through the pages of her diary. Looks in the back of her wallet. It will be in there somewhere, jotted down in biro on one of the little notepads that are always on the bar, courtesy of Gus Carter, the bookie next door.

'Don't worry!' I say to her, not wanting the moment to be lost in a paperchase. 'Just tell me how it starts. I'll probably recognise it.'

'It's a love poem but it's not the usual kind of love poem. It's the morning after and she's looking at him in the room . . .'

'Looking at his head asleep on the pillow and thinking it's like the head on an ancient coin?'

> 'and as remote
> > as those dead kings
> > > from my seeking eye.'

'No, he's not asleep. He's walking around the room and she's watching him . . .'

> 'this morning
> > he walks naked
> > > in front of me?'

'That's it!'

And we say the lines together, there in the middle of the crowded pub, with the Saturday evening drinkers pushing past us.

> this morning
> > he walks naked
> > > in front of me
> last night
> > slept easily
> > > by my side
> these more precious
> > than declaration
> > > or mating –

All the time I have been writing this journal, I have been questioning it. Is it too personal? Should I cut my own story out and just tell the story of the residency?

As I leave the Flying Horse, my hesitations vanish and I write it this way.

A Final Flourish
for Nancie in Paris

That Christmas,
we couldn't keep a straight face.

Even a kiss
was incongruous,

the sweet confluence
of the breath

a chortle of bronchitis.

I'm an old squeezebox, you said,
whose reeds have gone, a melodeon
with no melody.

That Christmas,
we were reduced to paper hats.

I held the wine glass to your lips
and then the cigarette.

Footsteps on a Path

The baby's feet
are not planted yet.

They nudge the earth
like windblown spores.

They could be kidney beans
or runner bean seeds.

The toes spill
like peas from a pod.

But look at Harry's
good foot, how it shifts

its grip, how it crampons
around the ice-axe

of his stick. The other
may be numb now,

may be swung
on a caliper, but how

that left one is rooted,
how it loves the earth.

The Workshop in the Quarry

Before we have set up
the primus stove, or opened
Environmental Art, they are away

over the first hillock, two boys
running down into a gully
that streams under them, stone-specked earth

glinting in a fresh wave
they have to dodge left or right
into willow scrub. Not far

—brushwood on spoilheaps
from the quarry's last working –
but far enough. They bend

and cut themselves a stick.
Half-rise, as if the body
had remembered another language,

or was poised, listening
for it. And set foot
in the hall of the forest.

101

Jack the Lad

'Jack ran away with the gypsies, you know.'

No one smokes now. Only voices
wreathe over the table, old stories
that hang in the air.

This has the colour of woodsmoke,
that magical blue.

'When was that, Jack?'

'When I were twelve.
I met these bairns with
a go-kart and they asked
where I lived. "Anywhere,"
I said, "and nowhere."'

Sharp-faced kid
in long shorts, Houdini
of the back lanes.

They taught him to handle horses,
to drive the fish-and-chip van
to Houghton Feast,
the pony and trap to Birtley
for fresh fireclay.
Bedded him down in the caravan,
snug with a relined stove.

'Six month I were with them
and never a bad word.'

What is as magical
as kindness?

Or simply as soap
and hot water?

'Best six months I ever had
– a bath every night!'

Shame lifted off
with the dirt, that
scab-kneed scutter
past the front steps.

He was walking tall
at the horse's head,
he was where he belonged,
when the paper said

they were going to drag the river
to find him.

No road home
was ever harder,

back from the gypsies
to the cruel stepmother.

The Spirit of Lumley Hall

'Time was,' he remembers,
it was all of a piece.

I dispensed Justice
to the miners of Madeley
as I might to the Masai
or the Solomon Islanders.

One dispensation
wherever the flag flew,
wherever there was a parade ground
and an Anglican church.

I remember the colliery band
on Empire Day, how the cornets
crew like cockerels. Sounds
ridiculous now. Small-town strutters.
Kings of the heap. But then
it was like a second sunrise.

Far off, in the rests
between tunes, cockcrow
would answer cockcrow,
quoits of sound
pitched by other bugles
over other towns, as the Day
flowed across country and on west
around the globe, gilding domes
and pediments and flat mud roofs,
Mogul palaces with mosaic pillars
and clapboarded back-country
courtrooms: High Courts
and Petty Sessions, Assizes
and District Commissioner's rounds,
a twenty-four-hour guard
on the turning earth.

I stood on my terrace,
two steps up from the High Street,
not exactly the Parthenon
but a humble third cousin,
built of red brick. Proportion,
that's what I had. Proportion.
The visible representative
of order. Do you remember
the chain of beacon-fires
at the start of the *Agamemnon*?
How they raced home the news
of the Fall of Troy, "torch to torch
. . . one long succession"? That's how
I saw myself: as one stage
in a long relay, handing on
the glimmer of a belief
from Fifth Century Athens
that the law can set us free,
there could be such a thing
as a community of equals,
governed only by law.'

The voice firms up, as if
you were his subaltern,
so late in the day . . .

But you are two hours on
down the sun's track,
in the heat and hush
of a long room. Here's
an ostrich-plumed hat
in a glass case. Here's
a cutaway coat with
a gold-braided collar.
And here are sketches
from the first days
of independence, for
African dress modelled
on the Roman toga.

After the Vintage Procession

*After the stutterers and the stallers
and the shudderers on four thin wheels,*

came the formation dance team of upright Hoovers,
the rumba troupe of twin-tub washing machines
and the shimmy of spin-driers,
came the Viennese waltz of two-door toasters,
one door flung back
as they swept into the turn.

*After the bread van in saffron
and the coal lorry in bottle green,*

came the clothes horses of the King's Troop
and the honour-guard of one-bar electric fires,
came the straight backs of the tallboys,
the overmantels and the hall hatstands,
all ushering in *Crown Imperial*,
the radiogram designed by Sir Edwin Lutyens.

*After the bull-roar of the Royal Enfield
and a gander's honk from the long-necked Riley,*

came the brrng! brrng! of the black lacquer telephone,
the ping of the egg-timer
and the buzz of the Teasmaid,
came a full set of door-chimes
playing
Love and Marriage, Love and Marriage,
Go Together like a Horse and Carriage.

The Country over My Shoulder

'All in ribbons and bows. All done up for the fair': that's what Eugenia
said when she looked at the English landscape. When I looked at the
Andes, I saw what she meant. Thousands of feet of rockfall. Three-
mile depths of blue air. Out of which mountains rise like razor edges
of cloud, distant as a daylight moon. It is humbling when the earth
shrugs off human endeavour, when a centuries-old Spanish colonial
town is no more than a scratch in the rock. Colombia is a frontier,
which has its dangers. I was there when the Drug War broke out. And
through the first massacres of the Guerrilla War. I watched Eugenia
paint out her grief and anger in condors (the emblem of Colombia)
like flak-torn Lancasters, bird skulls that were screeches of pain. But
what I miss, now that I'm back among the ribbons and bows, is the
sense of frontier and the spirit it engenders. A weight lifts off you once
you leave Europe, the weight of belonging to a dominant species.

An Accomodation

Penny plain
the crossing cottage

no rosebower trellis
not even a proper porch

just a curve of wood
that blinks back the rain

intimate as an eyelid

Working Through Resistance

– A DOUBLE ACT

for Borderline Printmakers and the children of
Longlands Primary School, Market Drayton

What can a lead pencil do?

Draw a leaden town,
all its bones and shadows,
the x-ray of its streets.

Creepy! Who wants the skeleton
of a house?

Trace it onto a screen and rub
with red ink. It turns to fire,
as if the bricks still glowed
from the kiln.

Who do you think I am?
Shadrach, Meschach and Abednego?

Or cut it out
of corrugated cardboard.
Stick on some cottonwool,
roll on some ink – yellow
and brown? – and put it
through the mangle.

Ouch!

A luminous mist
of beech and chestnut,
as if the house could turn
with the year and breathe
its colours out.
Honeysuckle smokes to seed
under the kitchen window.

Been at the wacky-baccy?
'Oh, to be a cloud
floating in the blue . . .'

Look, all these prints are
on fabric. Thread the machine
with embroidery twist
and run them through.

Trees are electricities,
live wires of red and green.

Water flies off a mill-wheel
in pulses of white and blue.

Roof tiles have the wingbeat
of migrating birds.

Goldfish scales, they run
through an octave of light.

Shall I bring you your bow
of burning gold? Build Jerusalem
here, in Market Drayton?

But heaven is like that.
Always down to earth.

Even the roots underground,
look, are bugle-beads.

Smokey

Gone to earth.

Laid to rest
in Frances' shawl
under the conifer

after so many journeys

greyfooted through grief
and love. Safe home
to the turn of the path

above the well.

                  Safe home
for the slip of a kitten
from the Slad Valley

a Sunderland tom straddled.

Safe home for the young queen
suckling in the kitchen cupboard
while Flash trembled on tiptoe,

anxious to become an aunt.

Safe home for the orphan mother
of a wandering son, fed from
the fish and chip van in Orcop

while Frances thinned to a swan's bone.

Safe home for the plaintive voice
in the garden at Tylluan Wen
after the cats' club had closed

and first Adam then Roger had wandered.

Safe home for *la gatica*, given
a fifth life in another garden,
another language, *¡Hola Miss Miss!*

and left to winter alone.

Safe home for the Lady
of Ladywell, for the Highland Wild Cat
who emerged from under the shed

with rolls of fat under her fur.

Safe home for the enquiring glance
from the well cover
and the long back reclining,

for shape-shifter and sundial.

Safe home for the snow-stepper,
flicking the crystals off each paw
as she went, for the reluctant crouch

and the flurry back indoors

to the lap of honour where, one paw
over the nose, one hare's foot
overhead, she was upside-down

with delight, my love,

these last four years, and
already safe, already
safe home.

Valentines
for Margaret

1 PRIMROSE

Nothing stronger
than this wash
of watercolour

the first panning
of gold
on the carpet

the sun's
indoor flowers
or you in your chair

soft as the first rose
the primerose
in its rock shelter

2 SPRING IS HERE
   (to the sound of Ben Webster)

First the touch
of the brushes

glistenings
and tricklings
of water under ice

then the south wind
of the bass

the small rain
of the piano . . .

Warm air ruffles
around a reed

and you unfurl
a scarf

unbutton a long glove
of midnight blue

shimmy and shrug off
a shoulder strap

gleam and escape me

full-bodied flower
on a single stalk
of breath

smoky rose

3 WILD RASPBERRY

A drop of colour
falling

translucent as a bead
of pomegranate

colour that knows
no withholding

that comes as blood
to the skin

all the possibilities
of overlay

everything the lips
will silkscreen

(even the Rothkos
of closed eyelids)

given away
in a blush

4 THE BOUQUET

Remember the third band
in the braid of your ring?
That was the luck of it,
wedding you to Ladywell?

All winter you have worked,
clearing nettles, shifting
ash heaps, opening up
the slope. Until the light

quickens to the light
of a lived-in place,
ground given the time and
trouble of love. No wonder

the primroses welled up
last spring – remember,
below the rhododendron? –
brimming for a bride.

5 A CHANCE OF THE LIGHT

The shadow of a hedge,
feather-perfect on the snow:

the brushwork in even bars,
as if pressed from the side
of the brush, and pressing out

a summer dust, a lilac shadow
I slide over the brown
of your shoulder, lift away

from the freckle on your breast.

Oyster Mushroom

Rarest of the esculents, its distribution
so wayward as to seem almost wilful,
it is sought in a kind of dance
along paths you can never retrace,
every step taken for you, and the woods
closing behind you with every step.
Just when you are lost, when the woods themselves
seem at a loss, it discloses itself,
a hidden fold, flower of the fork.
Chew softly, undressed or with a little yoghurt.

Two Poems from 'Presences of Jazz'

1 BECHET'S LOW NOTES

                    A boxer's shuffle
in the resin tray
                    before he climbs
into the ring
                    amber grains
beads of gloss
                    ground into
the foothold
                    he floats on

                    or a wall
he presses against
                    as he plays
the sledge
                    of each voice
through the dark
                    of a Texas jail
as they drive
                    their blues down

                    or a call
on the reed
                    so deep
the groundswell
                    of the wood
of the African
                    blackwood
answers more than
                    he could ask

A sandpiper's call
turning roofline
to shoreline

cornices
to the edge
of a quay

a mooring
on the estuary
of air

where a pigeon
skims itself
like a stone

and flocks of
egrets fold
into magnolias

as if time
had blossomed,
all the time

in the world
before the trumpet
rasps

and he struts
up the avenue
he's just blown away

cock-a-doodle-dandy

In All My Holy Mountain
poems in honour of Mary Webb
written for jazz settings by Nikki Iles

1 WESTERLY

It begins as a breath

a softness in the air
over the oakwoods

the first dustings of blue

*

brings a sea-change

the luminous shadow
of an Atlantic calm

close faraway light

*

catches the drift of

the stream, the wooded tumps,
rephrasing them in blues

finer than woodsmoke

*

takes the breath away

over the hillfort
in a blue that lifts

like a curlew's call

She wanders
the rosewalks of sunrise
frailer and brighter
than the rose of the briar
finds a path
beside the still waters
greener and paler
than the veins of a young beech-leaf
glimpses *a garden*
God might walk in
delicate as a moth

up at first light
for *the fascination of shadows*
almost as blue as chicory
still out at evening
to find them *richly blue,*
of the tint of a chaffinch's head

knows the hidden scents
the sweetness of woodruff
in a deep lane
the resins of agrimony
on a dusty road
even the characteristic odours
of the trees
the perfume thrushes smell

notices
the flock movements of flowers
how the white clover
folds into prayer at dusk
the wood-sorrel
wraps around the stalk before rain
the periwinkle
inclines from its fill of light
in the *pale shadow*
of a gesture . . .
as lovely, as inevitable
as the flight of wild swans
beating up the sky

117

                    cycles all day
unchaperoned
                    outrider of spring
entranced
                    and tireless
until the spring
                    she is lost
to the spring
                    lost to herself
in the parchings
                    of fever
unable to eat
                    or drink
or take anything
                    but an ice-cube
on the tongue

                    It is autumn
when she wakes
                    the autumn of
her twenty-first year
                    Wild raspberries
blush in the hedges
                    Sweet and white
the hazel nuts
                    plump in their shells
and she wakes
                    to protruding eyes
to the bulge
                    of Derbyshire neck

                    Then come
the high collars
                    the tulle scarves
and the enormous bows
                    then come
the wide-brimmed hats
                    and the trailing
wing of hair
                    then comes
the scurry
                    down the street

the wren's glance
                as she passes

                and then come
the phrasings
                in the third person
the prescriptions
                of her *little book*
of healing

                all the wildings
brought home
                and pressed
into the pages

                all the songs
sung over
                the chiff-chaff
with his two small notes
                like silver shears

and none sweeter
                than the tenuous notes
of the sedge warbler
                who sings for the sleepless
while night pales
                toward the dawn

3 FATHERLESS

When a stoop came
into his tall frame,

the world-tree bent.

When the amused eyes
lost their enquiry,

the stars were snuffed-out.

Gone was the guardian,
the moving lantern

at lambing time,

and the calm sensed
through fever, the presence

beside the sickbed.

As her brothers left
she saw him bereft

of his fatherhood,

watching his heaven
dwindle and darken,

and thought of the oaks

on Lyth Hill, old hulks
roped with honeysuckle,

and the wild cherry's

white pillars, where she'd
sat *in the very*

throne-room of white light.

4 THE WEDDING BREAKFAST
Never one
for the resonances
she was born to,

Miss Meredith
of The Grange,

she caught
the self-effacings
of border speech,

120

the withheld music
in the voices
of the cottagers

that disclaim themselves
as they rise, traces of
the language of heaven

in the intimate form
of address, *Come
thy ways in, my dear,*

and began to prepare
a table, to lay on
a feast: as a child

at Christmas dressing
a Tree for every
last child of the poor;

or as a girl quietly
bringing the tea with her
in a pony and trap.

Never so well-placed
as now, though, in
her bride's privilege,

in the ushering
of seventy guests
under a marquee:

all the old women
from Cross Houses, released
from the workhouse ward

for the day . . . old men
winkled out of shuts
and back lanes, herbalist

and organ-grinder . . . all
caught up in the twinkling
of an eye, a midsummer

day's dream, and set down
before pies and pickles,
syllabubs and jellies,

strawberries and cream . . .
and all of them eating
to her heart's content,

such bright music
of silver on china
they might have been

at table in the halls
of heaven, in one
of the many mansions.

5 THE HAUNTING

'What passing bells for those who die as cattle?'

Only the wash
of their voices
on the air

the singing
from troop-train windows
as they were shipped south

young men in their first flush

'Quicker their blood to earth
than to their wedding'

who left the ghost-cuts
of their spades
in the potato patch

glimmerings of twine
around raspberry canes
and pea sticks

the shine of their boots
on the roots
of the blackthorn

'After the revelling
there was silence'

a stilled voice
in the brimming
of the waterbutt

a stopped hand
in the rust
on the gatelatch

a lost stride
in the greening
of the wheelrut

The dead were walking
with the walking wounded

their hands hollowed
in the hands
around a match

their lips drawn
in the lips drawing
on the flame

their hunger crowding
to the brink
of the least thing

and she wove a woman
from the flower of men

supple as their hands
at the lambing, as their wrists
on the scythe

light as their step
on the haycart, as their pitching
of sheaves

direct as the line
of their furrow, as their speech
among themselves

        and set her to dance
on the potato patch

with the quicksilver
of the otter
before the poles cross

with the side-steps
of the hare
before she's worn down

with the heel-springs
of the deer
until the heart gives out

6 THE PART SONG

        'And Jim
telling me as my breast was soft as silk'

   – an old woman's voice,
just as she had imagined it,
the 'o' still opening into wonder
under the sibilants of age,

seventeen come Sunday . . .
the sweet perplexity
still unresolved, still fresh
off the skin . . . They soothe her,

these unfinished voices,
companionably puzzling

on the summer air . . . As if
there were no end to

astonishment, to her summons
out of solitude . . . No end
to his words on the tip
of her tongue, his silences

answering hers . . . No end
to the pencillings
in the margin, the criss-cross
of scripts, pairing like swifts

on the wing . . . Only such
a pause as she hears
in the voices, telling
their loves over . . . Sheep

cry . . . Shouts of haymakers
rise from the plain . . .
Cloud shadows
pass . . .

Notes

All the phrases in italics are taken from Mary Webb's own
writings. I am also indebted to Hilda Addison's memoir, *Mary
Webb*, and to Gladys Mary Coles's biography, *The Flower of
Light*.

Everyone will recognise the quotation from Wilfred Owen at
the beginning of 'The Haunting'. The other two quotations
are taken from *The Gododdin* of Aneirin, a sixth-century
Welsh lament for men lost in battle, in Tony Conran's trans-
lation.

Border Songs

engraved on glass screens
in the County Records & Research Centre, Shrewsbury

I

Ridgeway
to river crossing

hill trades with downland
lava flow with chalk outcrop

axeheads for arrowheads

Corndon's polished picrite
for the flints
of the Breckland

leaf-shaped
barbed and tanged

whatever
gives an edge

II

Behind the timber-lace
of ramparts
between the horns
of the gate

a honeycomb of huts
and granaries
the humdrum of looms

Behind their ditch
a family

with their hide racks
and hay trees

their boiling stones
and needle hones

who may survive

the charred timber
the burnt-out hive

III

It was their word
against ours

and we were
speechless

baa-baa-barians

who wore rain
and spoke fog

until one man
stood his ground

so tall
in his chains

they had to bite
their tongue

Caratacus

With his name
we raise our heads

Caer Caradoc
on every hill

IV

Measurements
in a legion's logbooks

lime burned
sand and gravel quarried

bricks baked
stones cut and carted

furnaces built
air ducts and aqueducts

until the idea
had streets at right-angles

colonnades
temples and law courts

baths for the body
a library for the mind

all lost on backwoodsmen
from north of the Rhine

who wonder at the work
of giants

V

Sweetness touches
another harp

Mine has only
bitter strings

Hwaet!
commands the scop
and strikes a single note

Silence spreads like smoke
under the high roof

He sings for the ring-giver
gleaming in his battle-gear
gloating in his wine

Where I must sing
is dark tonight

heb dan, heb wely

without fire
without bed

VI

Fathers at our backs

the mail-coat of memory
over our shoulders
the ring-braid of kin

how they fought Attila
in Vistula Wood

how the first Offa wielded
one sword against two

songs that would be ours
if sea-wolves did not sing them
as they sack the Severn burhs

if the Rome-Welsh
were not breaching the Dyke
with their own battlecries

Dawn is a whetting
of spears

so many songs
fight to be heard

VII

Towers rise
on their mottes
as seals sink
into their wax

The law is
a strange language
the land in fee

We are villeins
a standing army
of bordars and cottars
who fight the King's wars
or Mortimer's

Fortunes are made
and abbeys founded
towns planted
and burgages leased

We hardly weigh
in the scales

so many scruples
of FitzAlan's gold

VIII

Who can not wepe
com lerne of me

Eyes downcast
her sone
in her lappe laid

she looks across
the groined vault
of the transept

through the arches
of chapter house
and cloister

to back lanes
and open drains

childbed fever
and bloody flux

knowing how many angels
dance on the head
of a pin

how many sorrows
meet at the point
of an arch

IX

In the first
masquerade

the Queen is planning
marriage

and his armour is gilt
and blue

In the second

she is making peace
behind his back

From the Fortress
of Perfect Beauty
two cannons fire

one of sweet powder
one of sweet water

After Zutphen
he lies
with his thigh shattered

and knows death
by the smell

X

Slowly
Thy Kingdom comes

the art and mystery
of casting and moulding
of Iron Potts

after weeks of trial
with the keyhole stopped

Barr Iron
for the Forges
from Pit Coal pigs

after six days and nights
on the bridge of the furnace

Five Engine Cillinders
Cast Iron rails
an Iron Bridge

all from the refusal
of Friends

plain Friends

to turn cannon
from the Metal of Mars

XI

A flutelike call
from infinite distance

the rising spring
of a lapwing

the heart's systole
and diastole

driving back the cold
the endless sleep

among mammoth bones
in King Arthur's Cave

the song
of the family

the warmth
of belonging

wakes him in a hulk
off Punta Arenas

a Fourth Officer
wrapped in wool

XII

His last company

halted
against the shade
of a last hill

men he has led

through barrages
posted on fire-steps
huddled with in dug-outs

watched and watched over

until their blasphemies
have become
a kind of prayer

all that is human

all he can hear of hope
beneath *the shrill*
demented choirs

no glory in them

only a kind of prayer
he says over and over
all the courage he needs

to break ranks

Notes

I
The earliest Stone Age settlements were confined to flint-bearing areas such as
the Marlborough Downs and the Cambridgeshire Breckland. The discovery of
the technique of knapping flakes from a flint core, which they could carry with

them, enabled men to move out, colonise other areas, and discover new materials such as Picrite, a dark grey-green rock consisting mainly of chrysolite, a silicate of magnesia and iron found in lava. They shaped it into smooth stone axes, objects of beauty and power that were probably used in rituals and presented as gifts. It was the scattering of flints in the Shropshire hedgerows that enabled Miss Lily Chitty to trace the line of the Clee-Clun Ridgeway, which ran from Kerry Hill in Powys to the Severn Crossing at Bewdley (S.C. Stanford, *The Archaeology of the Welsh Marches*, revised edition, pp.5 and 25-7).

II

Details of the Hillfort at Caynham Camp, near Ludlow, and the Iron Age Farm at Bromfield are taken from Stanford, pp.52-7. A spindle whorl, a weaving comb and loom weights were found in the excavations of two Herefordshire hillforts, Croft Ambrey and Sutton Walls (Stanford, p.67). Further details of the Iron Age Farm appear in Volume 70 of the *Transactions of the Shropshire Archaeological and Historical Society*. Shropshire is unusual in having the remains of outlying settlements as well as hillforts.

III

Tacitus tells the story of Caratacus and the impression he made in Rome. The details Tacitus gives are two few for us to be sure where Caratacus made his last stand. He became a folk hero, like Arthur, whose name could dignify any hill. There is one Caer Caradoc on the Long Mynd and another above Bucknell. The Welsh *Caer*, like the English 'Chester' or '-.cester', is derived from the Latin *Castra*, a military camp.

IV

The street plan of Roman Wroxeter is so close to that of Roman Chester that Stanford suggests (p.96) it may have been laid out by a detachment from the Chester garrison, using measurements already in their logbooks. The Romans mixed so much lime in with their sand and gravel that their cement is virtually indestructible. The 'Old Work', the wall of an enormous exercise hall alongside the public baths, still stands eight metres high in the centre of Wroxeter. The baths catered for the mind as well as the body: the baths of Caracalla in Rome contained two libraries and a sculpture gallery. (Jérôme Carcopino, *Daily Life in Ancient Rome*, pp.285-6).

The Anglo-Saxons were a timber culture and could only marvel at the Roman remains, which they called *enta geweorc*, the work of giants. The impression of living among the ruins of a higher civilisation gave a distinctive melancholy to Anglo-Saxon poetry, which can be seen in *The Wanderer* and *The Ruin*, believed to be based on the ruins of Roman Bath.

Both poems can be found in *The Earliest English Poems*, translated by Michael Alexander (Penguin Classics, 1966).

V

Hwaet!, Listen!, was how the scop, or Anglo-Saxon bard, began his song. The details of the feast are taken from the glimpse in *The Ruin* of a 'high, horn-gabled' hall and warriors 'flushed with wine-pride'.

The refrain *heb dan, heb wely*, without fire, without bed, occurs in one of the earliest fragments of Welsh poetry, *Stavell Gyndylan*, or The Hall of Cynddylan, a series of ninth-century stanzas in which Heledd, a seventh-century princess of Powys, laments the death of her brother Cynddylan at the hands of the Angles and the destruction of his court at Pengwern, which has been variously identified as Wroxeter, the Wrekin, Shrewsbury, Baschurch or Bury Walls.

A translation by Tony Conran can be found in his anthology, *Welsh Verse* (Seren Books). David Jones makes a haunting use of the same refrain in his long poem, *The Sleeping Lord* (Faber, 1974), a consummate evocation of the Romano-British traditions of the Marches.

VI

Widsith, the earliest poem in the English language (and in any Germanic language) was probably composed in seventh-century Mercia during the reign of the Offa who built the Dyke. A mythic version of the history of the Angles before they came to England, it refers to the legendary battle between the Goths and the Huns *ymb Wistlawudu*, tells of the first Offa's duel on an island in the mouth of the Eider, and includes the 'Rome-Welsh' in its list of peoples. The Angles shared much of this history with the Vikings, who began to raid along the River Severn in the ninth century. Bridgnorth and Shrewsbury were two of the burhs, or fortified towns, built to hold them back.

For 'ring-braid' I am indebted to Michael Alexander's translation of *The Battle of Maldon*. Anglo-Saxon poetry is full of kennings, changes run on familiar phrases, such as 'swan's way' or 'whale road' for the sea. 'Ring-braid' is one of his kennings for the mail-coat. I use it as a metaphor for the cynn, the group of men, all more or less related, who gathered round a lord or 'ring-giver' and formed the basic unit of Anglo-Saxon society.

I have lifted 'Dawn is a whetting of spears' from the sixth-century Welsh poet, Taliesin, and filed it down for my own purposes. The original has a wider resonance. In Tony Conran's translation it reads 'His whetted spear the wings of dawn'.

VII

Norman power was based on a radical application of the feudal system. After the Conquest, William claimed the whole of England as his personal property. All land, even church land, was held from him 'in fee', in return for knight service. (R.H.C. Davis, *The Normans and their Myth*, p.107).

As lords were vassals, so men were villeins, holding their cottages and plots of land from the lord of the manor in return for labour and military service. Bordars (from the medieval Latin *borda*, a hut) and cottars (from the Anglo-Saxon *cotsaeta*, a cot-sitter) were the lowest ranks in the feudal system.

The Welsh Marches took some securing – over a hundred and fifty motte-and-bailey castles were built in Shropshire in the century after the Conquest –

and the Marcher Lords, such as the FitzAlans of Oswestry and Clun and the Mortimers of Wigmore, were granted a considerable measure of independence in return for defending them. (March is from the Anglo-Saxon *mearc*, a landmark or boundary.) Their lands were concentrated, so that they could quickly raise an army, and were virtually private kingdoms. A man could be fined for leaving the Marches without his lord's permission. Independence could lead to rebellion, witness the 'revolted Mortimer' of Shakespeare's *Henry IV Part 1* who joins forces with Owen Glendower.

Once the Marches were secure, lords and even abbots planted towns as a commercial speculation, renting out burgage plots around the marketplace. Richard's Castle is an example of a town that failed, Ludlow of one that succeeded.

VIII

The opening lines are taken from *Suddenly afraid*, an anonymous medieval poem in which the poet has a vision of the Virgin. The complete poem can be found in *A New Canon of English Poetry*, edited by James Reeves and Martin Seymour-Smith (Heinemann, 1967).

Norman England was the richest country in Europe because it was the most heavily taxed. It was this wealth that enabled the Normans to build our abbeys and cathedrals, and to undertake the experiments in architecture that led to the perfecting of the English Perpendicular style. When the central tower of Winchester Cathedral collapsed in 1107, they simply rebuilt it (Davis, p.121).

IX

The tournament of the Fortress of Perfect Beauty was held at Whitsun, 1581, to entertain the French commissioners who had come to negotiate Elizabeth's projected marriage to the Duke of Alençon. Philip Sidney was one of the four challengers who called themselves the Foster Children of Desire. According to Henry Goldwell's *A Briefe Declaration of the Shews*, he appeared 'in very sumptuous manner, with armour part blue and the rest gilt and engraven, with four spare horses having caparisons and furniture very rich and costly, as some of cloth of gold embroidered with pearl and some embroidered with gold and silver feathers very richly and cunningly wrought. He had four pages that rode on his four spare horses who had cassock coats and Venetian hose all of cloth of silver, laid with gold lace and hats of the same with gold bands and white feathers, and each one a pair of white buskins. Then had he a thirty gentlemen and yeomen and four trumpeters . . .'

He was less well supplied against the Spanish in the Netherlands. His troops had not been paid for four months and he had to send a messenger to 'my Lords of the Council' in England drawing their attention to 'the weak store of all sort of necessary munition'.

He still had a full suit of armour but, according to Fulke Greville, 'meeting the Marshall of the Camp lightly armed . . . the unspotted emulation of his heart, to venture without any inequality, made him cast off his cuisses, and so, by the secret influence of destiny, to disarm that part where God (it seems) had resolved to strike him.' His thigh was shattered by a musket ball.

He was given a hero's funeral: but the Queen was later to complain that he had wasted the life of a gentleman with a common soldier's fate. (Roger Howell, *Sir Philip Sidney The Shepherd Knight*, pp. 3-5, 85-8, 252-5, and **265**).

X

All the quotations are taken from Arthur Raistrick's history of the Coalbrookdale Company, *Dynasty of Iron Founders*.

The first quotation is from the bond drawn up between John Thomas and Abraham Darby I in January 1707. Between them they had perfected the art of casting pots in fine sand.

The second is from a letter written in 1775 by Abiah Darby, widow of Abraham Darby II, describing the trials her husband had made in 1749-50 to produce high-quality iron, fit for the forges of the nailers and locksmiths, from a coke rather than a charcoal furnace.

'Fire Engine' was the original name for a steam engine. One of Coalbrookdale's early successes was in casting iron 'cillinders' (the spelling used in the Company Accounts of 1724) rather than brass cylinders for the steam engines that drove the pumps in the mines. Wooden waggonways had been in existence for some time but the world's first iron rails were cast at Coalbrookdale, as, of course, was the world's first iron bridge.

Metallum Martis, the Metal of Mars, was the title of Dudley's early treatise on iron.

The Darbys, and most of their associates and employees, were strict Quakers, 'plain Friends', who wore Quaker costume, used 'thee' and 'thou' and kept apart from the world. Elizabeth Fry, the prison reformer, was brought up as a 'gay Friend' or worldly Quaker but discovered her vocation to be a strict Quaker while staying with the Darby family in Coalbrookdale.

Apart from a brief period when control had passed out of the Darbys' hands, the Coalbrookdale Company refused to turn cannon or to sell iron at an inflated price in time of war.

XI

In *Journey from Obscurity*, his memoirs of the Owen family, Harold Owen tells how 'the song of the family' came to him in an extraordinary dream when he was benighted in a freezing hulk in the South Atlantic.

The Palaeolithic remains in King Arthur's Cave, Whitchurch, were first excavated in 1871 (Stanford, pp. 12-16) and may well have been known to the Owen brothers. Wilfred was a frequent visitor to Shrewsbury Museum and to the excavations of Wroxeter, where he made a number of finds himself. Harold was taken along for his sharp eyes. Often it was Harold who made the find, only to cover it up so that Wilfred could rediscover it.

XII

I took my cue from a remark Wilfred Owen made in a letter to his mother in February 1918: 'There is a point where prayer is indistinguishable from blasphemy. There is also a point where blasphemy is indistinguishable from prayer. (Jon Stallworthy, *Wilfred Owen*, p.258). It made me think of *Apologia Pro Poemate Meo*, of the 'fellowships . . . wound with war's hard wire' and the beauty 'in the hoarse oaths that kept our courage straight'.

'Halted against the shade of a last hill' is the opening line of *Spring Offensive*. The 'shrill demented choirs' are taken from 'The shrill demented choirs of wailing shells' in *Anthem for Doomed Youth*.

In the Preface that he left in rough draft, Owen makes it clear that 'This book is not about heroes . . . nor anything about glory, honour, might, majesty, dominion, or power . . .

One of the losses the other poet, 'the enemy you killed, my friend', laments in *Strange Meeting* is that now 'None will break ranks, though nations trek from progress.